ACCOUNTS
MADE EASY

ACCOUNTS
MADE EASY

Rob Dransfield
and
Martin Coles

First published in 2001 by
Nelson Thornes Ltd
Delta Place
27 Bath Road
Cheltenham
GL53 7TH
United Kingdom

A catalogue record for this book is available from The British Library.

ISBN 0 7487 7017 8

02 03 04 05/10 9 8 7 6 5 4 3 2

Diagrams by Steve Ballinger, cartoons by Nathan Betts
Page make-up by Paul Manning

Printed in Great Britain by Scotprint

*The authors would like to thank Paul Manning and Sandy Marshall at Nelson Thornes
for their help in bringing this book to publication.*

Thanks also to Sheikh Abbas in Mauritius for sharing some of his ideas.

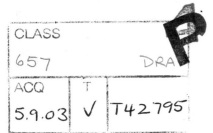

Contents

Unit 5: Ratio Analysis

Unit 6: Costs and Decision-Making

Introduction

This book has been written to help you to quickly develop a good understanding of the nature of finance and accounts and to enable you to use and interpret accounts.

We wrote the book because we know that a lot of students and managers struggle with this area. Often, students find it difficult 'to see the wood for the trees' – either because they are introduced to too many concepts too quickly, or because they are given confusing tasks which prevents them from developing an overview of the accounting process.

This book aims to help you develop a 'helicopter' view of accounts – enabling you to see from above the key structures and outlines of the accounting process. At the same time we have tried to make sure that the accounts are presented in a realistic way. We have not sought to oversimplify – if you want to understand how accounts work, you have to work at it.

Doctor Proctor is our vehicle for helping and guiding you through the key features of finance and accounts. We hope that you find him to be a helpful and sympathetic guide.

About the authors

Rob Dransfield is a Senior Lecturer in Business and Economics at The Nottingham Trent University. He has also worked at the University of Mauritius, MIE as an external examiner for accounts.

Martin Coles is Financial Controller of an AIM-listed company He is also a qualified teacher and lectured for several years in finance and accountancy at Tresham Institute.

How to Use This Book

As you work through the text, you'll find the following features to help you.

Key Ideas

These are some of the fundamental ideas on which finance and accounting is based.

You Must Know This

Terms and principles that you need to learn by heart and understand

Doctor Proctor Calculates

Learn these methods of calculation – you'll save yourself a lot of time!

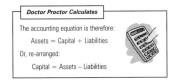

Distinguish Between...

Here you need to be able to explain the difference between one term or concept and another.

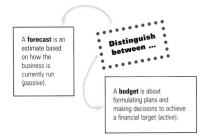

Doctor Proctor Outlines ...

Explanations of important themes and ideas in finance and accountancy

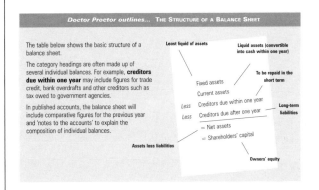

Activities

Practical accounting problems for you to puzzle out

Questions and Answers

Short, practical exercises to test your understanding

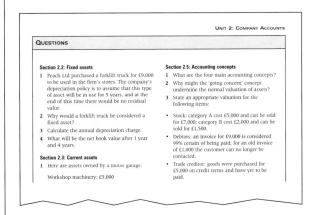

Topics covered in this unit

1.1 The Importance of Finance and Accounting
The role of the financial managers in organisations and why we all need to have some understanding of finance and accounts.

1.2 Accounting Records
The importance of keeping financial records. How managers can use these records to help control business activity.

This unit shows why a knowledge of finance and accounts is so important in helping you to understand how business works.

1.1 THE IMPORTANCE OF FINANCE AND ACCOUNTING

A key business objective is to generate wealth. To find out whether a business is achieving this financial objective we need to examine business results. These results are measured in money terms.

The role of the financial manager

Every business decision has a financial implication. Because of this, financial managers have an important part to play in every organisation.

Sometimes the power wielded by financial managers is resented by others. However, if organisations are to meet their financial objectives they will need to rely heavily on the wisdom of their financial managers.

Doctor Proctor outlines... FINANCIAL MANAGEMENT

Every aspect of business activity has a financial dimension – even things which seem to have little or nothing to do with financial management.

Let's look at two examples.

1 Staff welfare

The term 'staff welfare' refers to the way a company looks after its staff. This can include anything from sick pay provision to the organising of social events such as a staff party. Some firms are generous and caring, while others simply meet the minimum requirements laid down in employment law.

Every approach has its financial implications. For example, better welfare provision may result in a more dedicated and effective workforce who will

deliver greater financial benefits to the company. In this sense, a generous company could be said to be simply practising 'enlightened self-interest'.

2 Customer care

The term 'customer care' refers to a range of measures a company may take in order to meet the needs of its customers, including pre-sales advice and after-sales service.

Effective customer care programmes can be costly. But again, the increased cost of employing better-trained customer service staff or providing a more efficient returns, repair and maintenance service has to be weighed against greater customer loyalty. In the long run, this will considerably influence company pricing policy, and the company's ability to generate repeat and new business.

1.1 THE IMPORTANCE OF FINANCE AND ACCOUNTING

> ### Key Ideas 🔑
>
> **Finance: the language of business**

A knowledge of finance and accounts is essential to every member of an organisation.

Finance is the language of business, so it is a great advantage for any individual, from shop-floor worker to board member to be able to converse with colleagues in financial terms.

Every employee should be be able to understand financial information, to put forward a reasoned judgement for a particular course of action and to make decisions based on financial information.

There are three main areas of finance and accounting:

> If you have a good understanding of finance and accounts, you will be able argue convincingly with financial managers. Your argument will hold more weight because it will be backed up with a financial justification.
>
> Too often, managers who lack financial expertise lose arguments because what they believe to be right is not effectively translated into financial terms.
>
> Without a knowledge of finance and accounts, a non-financial manager may not have the confidence to defend their views.

1 **Treasury management** is concerned with making financial transactions and planning for how the business should be funded to pay for the resources it requires.

2 **Financial accounting** is concerned with the recording of financial transactions and the preparation of financial reports to communicate past financial performance.

3 **Management accounting** looks to the future, using a knowledge of past performance where relevant to aid the management of business.

1.2 ACCOUNTING RECORDS

Key Ideas 🔑

The importance of record-keeping

Keeping accounting records is a legal obligation for a company. Other important reasons for keeping these records are:

1. As a basis for financial reports, so that managers have information on which to run the business (**internal reporting**), and investors have information to monitor their investments (**published accounts**).
2. To control the financial resources of the business.

3. To provide the Inland Revenue and Customs and Excise with reliable information with which to assess the amount of tax due.

To simplify the process of keeping records, financial transactions are **coded**. Codes can be used for various types of transaction including:

- sales
- purchases
- payments to employees

Using these codes makes it easy to group similar transactions, and to make calculations based on them. **Account codes** are created for items of income and expenditure that are common across the business. **Business function** or **location codes** allow figures to be analysed in terms of profit centres or cost centres.

Doctor Proctor outlines... USING ACCOUNT CODES

Here's an example of how a business may use codes to record a business transaction:

Cost centre code (e.g. to identify a department)

Account code (to identify type of transaction)

678/1234

So if an extract from the code list looked like this:

Cost centre code	Description	Account code	Description
120	Sales: North	3001	Wages & Salaries
121	Sales: South	3002	Motor vehicle expenses
122	Sales: East	3003	Subsistence
123	Sales: West	3004	Entertainment
124	Sales office	3005	Training
		3006	Stationery
		3007	Meetings
		3008	Sundries

– wages for the eastern sales area would be coded **122/3001**.

A code structure enables flexible reporting of financial transactions. For example, the total of all transactions on **3001** account represents the business's total wages bill. Coded transactions can also be analysed by department. The total of account codes with cost centre **122** gives the cost of running the sales team in the East, analysed by type of expenditure.

1.2 ACCOUNTING RECORDS

Key Ideas

How financial records give control

Financial managers need records in order to control financial resources.

Individuals can memorise many facts without necessarily writing them down, but the corporate memory has to be based on records of what has occurred, and these records must be accurate, up to date, and available to everybody who needs them.

The need for records

Without accurate record-keeping, assets such as company cars or PCs may be vulnerable to theft or pilfering, or may be underused simply because employees do not know they exist or where to find them.

In the same way, businesses must have records of the amounts owed to them and the amounts they owe to others, in order to carry out effective financial management.

If no records are kept of cash received and cash paid out, mistakes will be made, fraud will go unchecked and financial planning will become impossible.

Doctor Proctor says: *Keep accurate accounting records!*

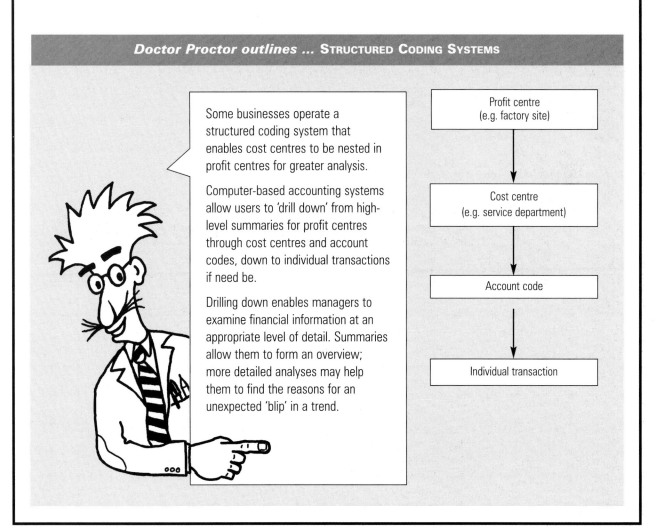

Doctor Proctor outlines ... STRUCTURED CODING SYSTEMS

Some businesses operate a structured coding system that enables cost centres to be nested in profit centres for greater analysis.

Computer-based accounting systems allow users to 'drill down' from high-level summaries for profit centres through cost centres and account codes, down to individual transactions if need be.

Drilling down enables managers to examine financial information at an appropriate level of detail. Summaries allow them to form an overview; more detailed analyses may help them to find the reasons for an unexpected 'blip' in a trend.

Profit centre
(e.g. factory site)

↓

Cost centre
(e.g. service department)

↓

Account code

↓

Individual transaction

This unit gives you an overview of the main types of accounts and their various components and headings.

Topics covered in this unit

2.1 USERS AND PURPOSES OF COMPANY ACCOUNTS

Key Ideas 🔑

Who needs company accounts?

Different individuals and groups make use of accounts because they have a stake in how the company is run – these are the **users**.

These users will use the accounts in different ways. These are the **purposes** for which accounts are used.

Dr Proctor says:

'You Must Know This!'

Stakeholders in a business need to have access to accurate, up-to-date information about its performance via the company report and accounts.

Doctor Proctor outlines... COMPANIES AND STAKEHOLDERS

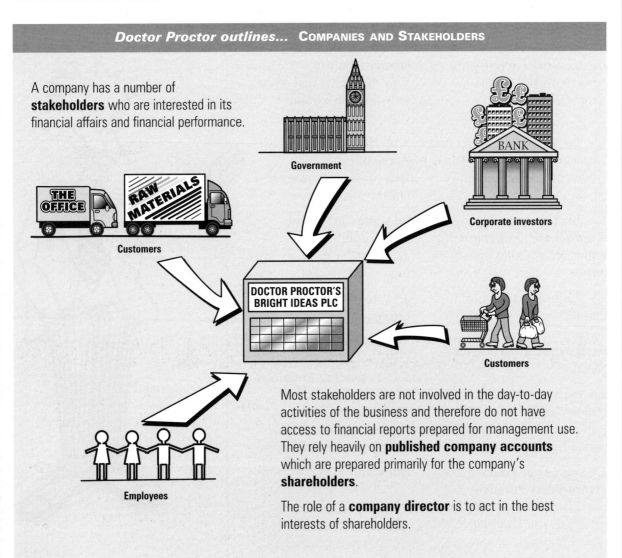

A company has a number of **stakeholders** who are interested in its financial affairs and financial performance.

Government

Corporate investors

Customers

Customers

Employees

Most stakeholders are not involved in the day-to-day activities of the business and therefore do not have access to financial reports prepared for management use. They rely heavily on **published company accounts** which are prepared primarily for the company's **shareholders**.

The role of a **company director** is to act in the best interests of shareholders.

2.1 USERS AND PURPOSES OF COMPANY ACCOUNTS

Key Ideas 🔑

Shareholder accounts

The shareholders' main concern is with the directors' stewardship of the company.

The focus of the annual report and accounts is therefore on:

- the **net wealth** of the company

- **financial performance**, measured in terms of the extent to which shareholders' wealth has been enhanced, with prominence given to the **profit from operating activities**

- **solvency**, with emphasis on the cash balance and the ability of the company to generate cash receipts in order to meet its current and future obligations

- the **directors' benefits**, including salaries and other benefits. Stakeholders need to ensure that these reflect the achievements of the directors and their value to the company.

These accounts need to be presented in such a way as to ensure that proper comparison can be made between different periods (to highlight **trends**), and so that the performance of different companies can be compared (**benchmarking**).

Shareholder accounts need to focus on key questions such as:

Is the company solvent?

If so, how much is it worth?

Can it meet present and future financial obligations?

How well is it performing and what are its financial prospects?

How much are the directors receiving in salaries and other benefits?

Doctor Proctor outlines... ACCOUNTS FOR OTHER STAKEHOLDERS

As well as shareholders, other stakeholders have an interest in the company accounts:

- **Customers** want to have confidence in the financial stability of the company to ensure continuing supplies.

- **Suppliers** are interested in their customers' solvency to ensure they get paid.

- **Employees** want to know that the employer is financially stable and able to offer a secure future. If profits are good, they may be encouraged to press for wage increases, bonuses or share options.

- **Government** needs to be able to assess tax liabilities on the basis of published financial information.

2.2 FIXED ASSETS

An important element in the company accounts is the valuation of the business's fixed assets. These can range from financial investments to premises, plant and equipment.

Dr Proctor says:
'You Must Know This!'

Fixed assets are the 'tools of the trade' that enable a business to generate wealth, and to function on a day-to-day basis. They are **not** purchased for resale to the customer.

Doctor Proctor outlines... TYPES OF FIXED ASSET

There are three main categories of fixed asset:

- tangible
- intangible
- investments.

1 Tangible fixed assets are physical things that you can touch and see. They include:

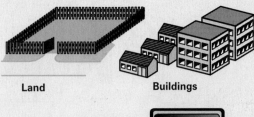

Land   Buildings

Machinery   Computers

Vehicles

2 Intangible fixed assets are non-physical items such as research and development and the **goodwill** of acquired businesses.

Example

A plumbing business is sold for £100,000, made up as follows:

Fixed assets	£50,000
Stock	£20,000
Goodwill	£30,000

The **goodwill** is the value placed on the good name of the business. A business with an established name and reputation will always have an advantage over a start-up. Research and development expenditure – for example, to develop a new product – is a payment made today in order to reap reward at some point in the future.

3 Investments are classified as fixed assets if they are long-term shareholdings in associated companies. Again, these help to secure the long-term future of the business.

2.2 FIXED ASSETS

Key Ideas

How fixed assets depreciate

In order to present an accurate picture of a company's financial status, the company accounts need to reflect the reduction in value of its fixed assets. There are a number of ways in which this can be done.

The value of a fixed asset such as a company car can decrease quite rapidly over a period of time.

This fall in value is accounted for by **depreciation** of tangible fixed assets and **amortisation** of intangible fixed assets.

Doctor Proctor outlines... ACCOUNTING FOR DEPRECIATION

There are a number of ways of calculating the fall in value of fixed assets. The most common is the **straight line method**.

According to the straight line method, depreciation is calculated as follows

Doctor Proctor Calculates

Annual depreciation/amortisation =

$$\frac{\text{Cost of asset} - \text{Residual value}}{\text{Economic life in this business}}$$

The value of a fixed asset at any point in time is called its **net book value**.

Net book value =

Cost of asset − Accumulated depreciation to date

The **cost** of an asset includes the purchase price, cost of installation, delivery to site, etc.

Residual value is the estimated amount to be received when the asset is eventually disposed of.

The **economic life** is the typical length of time period an asset of this type is held by the business.

(Any difference between the net book value and what the asset actually sells for will be counted as a profit or a loss).

Example

- A motor vehicle cost £13,000. It is expected to fetch £4,000 when it is disposed of in 3 years' time.

- Depreciation per year = (£13,000 − £4,000)/3 years = £3,000.

- Therefore after 1 year, the net book value of the vehicle is £10,000. After 2 years its net book value is £7,000, and after 3 years its net book value is £4,000.

2.2 FIXED ASSETS

The value of a fixed asset at any point in time is called its **net book value**.

Net book value is calculated as:

Cost of asset *less* accumulated depreciation to date

Doctor Proctor outlines... A FIXED ASSETS SCHEDULE

A **fixed assets schedule** in the accounts of a company analyses total 'net book value' in two ways:

1 between cost and accumulated depreciation

2 according to different types of fixed assets in use.

Example

	Property	Machinery	Motors	Total
			£000s	
Cost 1 January	2,000	1,000	500	3,500
Additions		200	150	350
Disposals			200	200
Cost 31 December	2,000	1,200	450	3,650
Depreciation 1 January	500	400	250	1,150
Charge for year	100	50	100	250
Disposals			150	150
Depreciation 31 December	600	450	200	1,250
Net book value 31 Dec Yr 2	1,400	750	250	2,400
Net book value 31 Dec Yr 1	1,500	600	250	2,350

2.3 CURRENT ASSETS

Key Ideas

Defining current assets

Current assets are assets that arise from, or are required for, the everyday trading of the business.

In practice, any asset that is not a **fixed** asset is a **current** asset.

All assets provide future economic benefits.

For a trading company involved in the purchase of goods for resale, the typical **cycle of funds** tied up in current assets is:

Debtors
(= IOUs for goods sold on credit)

Cash

Stocks

Doctor Proctor outlines... STOCKS, DEBTORS AND CASH

Stocks

Stocks consist of costs involved in providing goods or services to customers. There are three categories of stocks for manufactured goods:

1 **Raw materials** are goods in their original state purchased from outside suppliers – e.g. coal, iron ore, etc.

2 **Work-in-progress** refers to goods that are not fully made.

3 **Finished goods** are products that are ready for sale.

Debtors
(= IOUs for goods sold on credit)

Debtors
In commercial transactions most sales are made on credit – typically 30 to 60 days after sale. **Debtors** are customers of the business who have taken goods on credit.

Cash

Cash
Cash is a current asset because it is a resource that helps a business to meet its obligations to suppliers and employees in the short term.

2.3 CURRENT ASSETS

Key Ideas 🔑

Other current assets

Property rent paid in advance

Stocks and shares owned by the firm

Current assets are assets that arise from, or are required for, the everyday trading of the business, such as stocks, debtors and cash.

Other current assets include:

- **Prepaid expenses**. These are expenses that have been paid in advance.

  For example, if rent of £3,000 is paid on 1 April for the next three months, an asset is created. This is because future periods will benefit from the property's use. Over the next three months the value of the 'prepayment asset' will gradually decline: it will be worth £2,000 at the end of April and £1,000 at the end of May.

- **Investments** can also be categorised as current assets if they fail to satisfy the criteria for fixed assets. Hence, government bonds that are held to maximise interest receivable from surplus cash qualify as current assets. So do shares in other companies held for speculative reasons.

Doctor Proctor outlines... HOW TO CALCULATE CURRENT ASSETS

You can calculate the total value of current assets by adding together the various items shown here.

Example

Illustration of a 'current assets' section of company accounts:

	£000s
Stocks	900
Debtors	1,100
Investments	500
Cash	200
	2,700

2.4 LIABILITIES

Key Ideas 🔑

Defining liabilities

Liabilities are defined by the accountancy profession's Financial Reporting Board as:

'obligations of an entity to the transfer of economic benefits as a result of past transactions or events'.

For example, take the case of a printer who buys paper and agrees to pay the supplier in 30 days' time. Here a liability has been created, because there is a requirement to transfer economic benefit in the form of cash after, say, 30 days.

Liabilities = Amounts owed BY the business

Distinguish Between ...

Assets = Amounts owed TO the business

Doctor Proctor outlines... TYPES OF CREDITOR

In general **creditors** fall into three main categories:

1   **Sources of finance**: when debt is used to help finance the business (see **2.6, Sources of Finance**)

2   **Trade creditors:** for example, when goods and services are obtained on credit and payment is deferred

3   **Other creditors**: these might include Customs and Excise and The Inland Revenue, The company may also have obligations to shareholders if dividends have been declared but not yet paid.

2.4 LIABILITIES

The three types of liabilities described on page 15 are quite easy to account for because they can be quantified with reasonable certainty.

For example, the value of a loan agreement is set out in clear repayment figures, and the payment for goods supplied on credit is clearly set out on an invoice.

However, there are other liabilities which cannot be quantified so easily …

Doctor Proctor outlines... PROVISIONS AND ACCRUALS

When the value of a liability is hard to quantify, an accountant will create a **provision** – sometimes referred to as an **accrual**.

In some cases the accrual can be calculated relatively easily, such as when an electricity company takes an estimated meter-reading based on the customer's last bill.

In other cases, there is much less certainty – for example, when a company has to predict the future cost of repairing or replacing goods sold under guarantee.

To understand how liabilities affect the financial well-being of the business it is useful to know *when* creditors are required to be repaid. Financial reports do this by distinguishing between creditors due for repayment *within* one year and those due *after* one year.

Example

The listing of creditors for a company typically looks like this:

Creditors due for payment within one year	£000s
Bank overdraft	470
Trade creditors	550
Corporation tax	250
Other taxes and social security	150
Accruals and deferred income	70
Proposed dividend	250
	1,740

2.5 VALUING ASSETS AND LIABILITIES

Key Ideas

Assessing the true value of a business

To ensure that financial reports of a business state the true value of a business and reflect the amount of wealth created in a particular accounting period, it is vital that the value of an organisation's assets and liabilities is set out accurately.

Example

A courier business starts up with £15,000 in the bank. Of this, £14,000 is used to purchase two motorbikes.

After one year of trading, the business continues to own the bikes, has £5,000 in the bank and is owed £1,000 for its last job.

The value of the business critically depends on the valuation of the bikes and on the amount owed to it.

View 1

Assuming that the owner has not taken money out of the business, and that the business value is measured purely in cash terms, a 'loss' of £10,000 has been incurred as there was £15,000 and now there is only £5,000.

View 2

The maximum value of the business is £20,000 (14,000 + 1,000 + 5,000) assuming full value of the bikes and the debtor. This implies a 'profit' of £6,000.

In reality the bikes are worth less now than when they were first purchased, and there is always a risk, however small, that the debtor will not pay in full.

So, in order for the accounts of businesses to have meaning, and for ease of comparison with other businesses, there must be clearly defined rules for valuing assets and liabilities, whatever their form.

A number of 'accounting concepts' have therefore been developed to ensure that the accounts of different businesses are prepared and presented consistently (*see page 18*).

2.5 VALUING ASSETS AND LIABILITIES

Key Ideas

Accounting concepts

The 'Prudence' concept

Gains should be recognised only when they are reasonably certain. In contrast, losses should be provided for as soon as there is a 50% chance of their being incurred.

Prudence dictates that, when in doubt, assets should be valued at the lower end of the probable range, whereas liabilities should be pessimistically valued at the higher end of the probable range.

The 'Accrual' or 'Matching' concept

Revenues and expenses should be recognised as they are earned or incurred, and not as money is received or paid.

This concept is at the heart of business accounting and is what makes it different from a mere listing of transactions, as on a bank statement.

For example, when a sale is made, the profit is recognised whether the customer pays in cash or at some future date.

At the same time, a sale on credit causes a depletion in stock, but also creates an asset in the form of a debtor.

The aim here is to reflect the changing net value of the business's total assets and liabilities. This is a much more accurate way to measure the financial performance of a business than simply to record a change in the cash balance alone.

The 'Going Concern' concept

This assumes that a business will continue trading for the foreseeable future.

This test can significantly affect the valuation of a business's assets and liabilities. If for some reason the business looks likely to cease trading – for example, if poor trading performance is creating cash flow difficulties – it may have to sell off assets at significantly below the normal selling price. In this event, the prudence concept will require stocks and other assets to be marked down to a reduced net realisable value.

Similarly, if a business is unable to fulfil its contractual obligations –for example, to pay rent on its premises – it will need to create a provision for future liabilities. These liabilities arise as a direct result of the business's failure to meet the 'going concern' requirement.

The 'Consistency' concept

This requires that items of a similar nature should be accounted for on the same basis from one period to the next.

This makes it possible to compare financial performance over different time periods.For example, if a company car is depreciated over 4 years during one accounting period, it should continue to be depreciated in this way (over the 4 years) in the next and future periods.

2.5 VALUING ASSETS AND LIABILITIES

Applying accounting concepts

Accounting concepts are easier to understand when they are applied to real situations.

On page 18 we introduced a range of important accounting concepts.

Now let's look at how those concepts can be applied when valuing specific types of business asset.

Doctor Proctor outlines... METHODS OF VALUING ASSETS

Stocks

Stocks can be valued:

*   on the basis of what they cost the business to acquire or manufacture

*   on the basis of the price they could be sold for, less selling costs (net realisable value).

In accordance with the prudence concept, the lower of the two valuations is taken, i.e. they are valued at the lower of costs or net realisable value.

Debtors

Debtors (amounts owed by customers) are valued according to the amounts expected to be received from customers. This is calculated by taking the amounts invoiced to customers but not yet paid, and deducting a provision in respect of bad or doubtful debts. This usually involves reviewing the amounts outstanding and assessing the likely risk of non-payment.

Fixed assets

Fixed assets are valued at the lower of:

*   net book value (cost less depreciation)

*   their 'recoverable value'.

The **recoverable value** is the greater of:

*   the value created by using the asset

*   the asset's market value if sold.

These rules have developed because:

*   there is a requirement to match the depletion of value of the assets to the periods that will enjoy their benefit (**matching concept**)

*   because over the life of an asset, circumstances and expectations change, and this requires any decrease in value to be recognised immediately (**prudence concept**).

In most cases, an asset's calculated 'net book value' is the appropriate valuation.

Liabilities

Liabilities are recognised:

a) when a transaction creates an obligation to pay (**accruals concept**)

b) when there is some question whether the obligation will be met, or over the sum involved (**prudence concept**).

The valuation of the liability should be based on an actual or reasonable estimate of the amount to be paid. In the case of product guarantees, for example, the probability and average value of future claims (based on the prudence concept) arising from past sales (accruals concept) would have to be estimated from historical claims data.

2.6 SOURCES OF FINANCE: OWNER'S CAPITAL

Key Ideas

Owner's capital

The owners of a business are the ultimate risk-takers. Whilst they may make significant financial gains, they also risk losing the capital they have invested.

In a 'sole trader' or 'partnership', the one owner or partners provide the 'owner's capital' for the business.

'Incorporated businesses', known as **limited companies**, are legal entities and are separate from their owners. Here, the capital contributed by the owners is divided into 'shares' and the owner is called a **shareholder**.

Dr Proctor says:

'You Must Know This!'

The distinction between a private limited company (**ltd**) and a public limited company (**plc**) is that a plc can offer its shares to the general public, whereas the methods of issuing shares in a private company are restricted.

Plcs listed on the stock exchange gain a number of additional advantages, including;

- easier access to funds
- enhanced reputation
- increased share prices, as there is a ready market for the company's share capital.

Well-known companies listed on the Stock Exchange include Rolls Royce, Marks & Spencer, Stagecoach, BP and Marconi.

Doctor Proctor outlines... Share Trading

How are shares bought and sold?
A share in a limited company is a **tradeable security** which (subject to certain restrictions) can be bought and sold without directly affecting the business itself.

Unless it is a new issue of shares, the proceeds pass from seller to buyer without cash implications for the business. This enables investors to release their money when they need to, but has the advantage of not affecting the business's ability to trade.

Limited liability
Another consequence of this legal distinction between a business and its owners is that shareholders enjoy what is called **limited liability**. The maximum amount they can lose in the business is the amount they paid for the shares that they hold.

2.6 SOURCES OF FINANCE: OWNER'S CAPITAL

Key Ideas

Types of share

There are two main types of share: ordinary and preference. Each offers different rights to **dividends** (returns) and capital repayment.

Doctor Proctor outlines... ORDINARY AND PREFERENCE SHARES

Ordinary shares

Holders of ordinary shares are entitled to a share in the profits of the business after all other investors have been paid their dues. They are able to vote at general meetings of the company and to exert influence in direct proportion to the number of shares they hold.

Items requiring shareholder authorisation include:

- the appointment of the board of directors

- the amount of profits distributed by way of dividend to the shareholders

- the issue or repurchase of share capital.

Equity capital

Ordinary share capital is often called 'equity capital' and can be likened to owner's equity in a private house. Equity for the householder is the difference between the value of the house and the mortgage secured against it. In the case of a company, equity (the value of the ordinary shares) represents the difference between the value of assets owned by the business and the value of any outstanding loans and liabilities to other parties.

Preference shares

Holders of preference shares are entitled to receive a fixed dividend out of profits before payment is made to ordinary shareholders. But they usually have no voting rights, and so have less influence on company policy.

Issued capital

The number and nominal value of the shares actually issued to shareholders

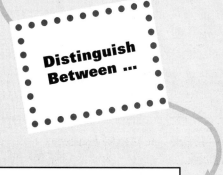

Distinguish Between ...

Authorised capital

The maximum number of shares the directors can issue according to the company's Memorandum of Association (a legal document drawn up when a company is established).

Example

	£000s
Assets: fixed and current	2,000
Liabilities	500
Equity	1,500

2.7 SOURCES OF FINANCE: THIRD-PARTY FINANCE

Key Ideas

Third-party finance

Funds provided by third parties come in a variety of forms. They are used by businesses for a range of different purposes, and terms of repayment vary according to the needs of the investor and the company.

Large amounts of business finance are provided by investors who do not want to take the risk of becoming a shareholder in a company.

These **third-party investors** include banks, insurance companies and pension funds, who for some of their investments at least, require stable income and greater security for their capital investment.

Doctor Proctor outlines... LOAN STOCK

The basic principle is that a loan is made to the company in accordance with terms set out in a certifying document. Typically, loan stock involves a fixed rate of interest and is repaid (redeemed) by the company on a predetermined date.

Sometimes loan stock is 'secured' on specified assets of the business in case the company runs into financial difficulties.

Example

An 8% debenture of £100 dated 1 November 2008 requires the company to pay £8 a year to the debenture-holder until 2008 when the capital sum of £100 must be repaid.

'Convertible' debentures are another attractive option for investors as they can be converted into shares at some future date and at a predetermined price. Debenture-holders therefore have fixed income in the short term with the possibility of capital gains at low risk in the long term.

Loan stock : how it works	
Loan period	Medium- to long-term*
Nature of finance	Financial securities that can be traded in the same way as a company's shares
Commonly known as	'loan stock', 'debentures' or 'company bonds'

* Key to loan terminology

Long-term   =   Over 5 years
Medium-term   =   1–5 years
Short-term   =   Up to 12 months

2.7 SOURCES OF FINANCE: THIRD-PARTY FINANCE

Key Ideas

Third-party finance (cont'd)

Popular sources of third-party finance for business are **banks** (for loans and overdrafts) and **finance houses** (for hire purchase)

Doctor Proctor outlines... BANK FINANCE AND HIRE PURCHASE

Banks are risk-adverse and, as well as requiring detailed business plans, will generally not lend more than the owners are putting into the business themselves. Security is also usually required. In the case of small businesses, this is often in the form of a personal guarantee secured by the personal assets of the major shareholders.

Bank finance: how it works	
Loan period	Short, medium or long-term
Nature of finance	A range of financial products provided by clearing banks. Includes overdrafts, loans, mortgages, sale and leaseback

Types of bank finance

- **Bank loans** are taken out for a fixed period with repayment being either in instalments or in full at the end of the term.

- **Overdrafts** are a more flexible form of finance. However, whilst interest is only charged on debit balances, amounts are legally repayable on demand.

- **Mortgages** are loans secured by land and buildings and are an exception to the general rule that banks do not provide long-term finance. The funds provided may be used to purchase the property, or in the case of property already owned, to provide security for a loan which is being used for some other purpose.

- **Sale and leaseback** is another form of finance for land and buildings. This involves the business selling its freehold property to an investment company, and then leasing it back over a predetermined period of time.

Hire purchase (HP)

Hire purchase allows the business to use an asset without having to find the money immediately. A finance house buys the asset from the supplier and retains ownership of it until the business has made the payments required under the hire purchase agreement. At the end of the HP agreement, ownership of the asset passes to the business.

Hire purchase: how it works	
Loan period	Medium-term
Nature of finance	Items are hired until a final payment is made, at which time they are fully owned by the purchaser

2.7 SOURCES OF FINANCE: THIRD-PARTY FINANCE

Key Ideas 🔑

Third-party finance (cont'd)

Leasing, **factoring** and **trade credit** are common sources of external finance for a business.

Doctor Proctor outlines... LEASING, FACTORING AND TRADE CREDIT

Leasing

Leasing works in the same way as hire purchase in that a finance house (the lessor) allows the business (the lessee) to use an asset without having to buy it outright. The real distinction between the two forms of finance is that leasing does not confer an automatic right to eventual ownership. It is a very popular form of finance for company vehicles, office equipment and factory machinery.

There are two types of lease:

• An **operating lease** is a rent agreement for a short period of time relative to the asset's useful life. For example, in the case of a car, a two-year agreement is fairly typical

• A **finance lease** tends to run for longer. The agreement will cover most of the asset's economic life and so payments under the agreement will, like HP, exceed the cash price of the asset.

Leasing: how it works	
Loan period	Medium-term
Nature of finance	Items are hired on an ongoing basis

Factoring

A major problem for many businesses is the length of time taken by customers to pay – the **credit period**. Typically this is 30–60 days, and in some cases considerably longer. Factors provide finance

Factoring: how it works	
Loan period	Short to medium-term
Nature of finance	Finance against a business's trade debt

against a business's trade debt by advancing up to 80% of the value of the invoices outstanding, with the remainder payable as and when customers pay at the end of their credit periods. Factors receive interest on the amounts they advance. They also charge an administration fee for taking over the credit control function of a business.

Trade Credit

Suppliers are a valuable source of finance for many businesses. Just as the business may give credit to its own customers, the firm may be able to negotiate credit terms with its suppliers. Credit terms are typically 30 days from date of supply or 30 days from the end of the month following the month of delivery, i.e. 30–60 days.

Trade Credit: how it works	
Loan period	Short-term finance (30–60 days from date of supply)
Nature of finance	Credit period before items purchased on credit must be paid for

2.8 THE BALANCE SHEET

Key Ideas

'Balancing' the balance sheet

A balance sheet must balance.
Assets and liabilities are continuously changing with business activity. For example, the purchase of stock increases stock values and the amounts owed to suppliers.

To understand the financial position of the business, it is necessary to 'freeze' the values of financial components at a certain point in time. These values, or **balances**, are used to construct a balance sheet which shows how the owners' equity is represented by the various categories of assets and liabilities.

Dr Proctor says:
'You Must Know This!'

Business accounting is based on the **separate identity** concept. This means that business finances are separated from the personal financial circumstances of the business owners.

Doctor Proctor Calculates

The accounting equation is therefore:

Assets = Capital + Liabilities

Or, re-arranged:

Capital = Assets − Liabilities

Doctor Proctor outlines... THE STRUCTURE OF A BALANCE SHEET

The example on the right shows the basic structure of a balance sheet.

The category headings are often made up of several individual balances. For example, **creditors due within one year** may include figures for trade credit, bank overdrafts and other creditors such as tax owed to government agencies.

In published accounts, the balance sheet will include comparative figures for the previous year and 'notes to the accounts' to explain the composition of individual balances.

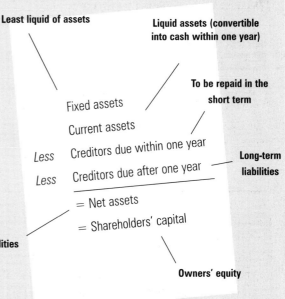

Least liquid of assets

Liquid assets (convertible into cash within one year)

To be repaid in the short term

Fixed assets

Current assets

Less Creditors due within one year

Less Creditors due after one year

Long-term liabilities

= Net assets

= Shareholders' capital

Assets less liabilities

Owners' equity

2.8 THE BALANCE SHEET

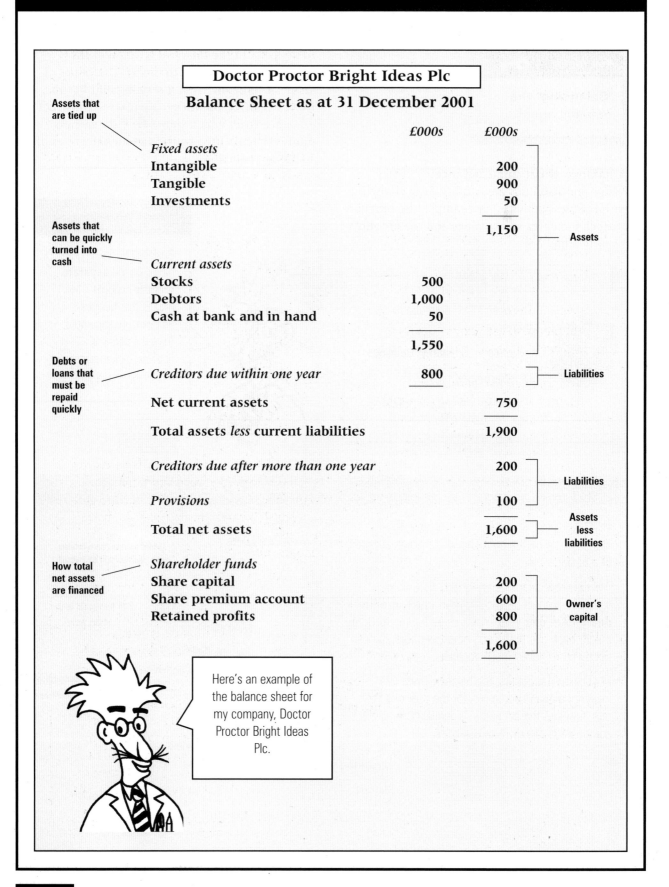

Doctor Proctor Bright Ideas Plc

Balance Sheet as at 31 December 2001

	£000s	£000s	
Fixed assets			
Intangible		200	
Tangible		900	
Investments		50	
		1,150	Assets
Current assets			
Stocks	500		
Debtors	1,000		
Cash at bank and in hand	50		
	1,550		
Creditors due within one year	800		Liabilities
Net current assets		750	
Total assets *less* current liabilities		1,900	
Creditors due after more than one year		200	Liabilities
Provisions		100	
Total net assets		1,600	Assets less liabilities
Shareholder funds			
Share capital		200	
Share premium account		600	Owner's capital
Retained profits		800	
		1,600	

Assets that are tied up

Assets that can be quickly turned into cash

Debts or loans that must be repaid quickly

How total net assets are financed

Here's an example of the balance sheet for my company, Doctor Proctor Bright Ideas Plc.

2.9 REPORTING CHANGES IN OWNER'S EQUITY

The capital (or *equity*) that shareholders have invested in the business changes directly with any change in net assets (assets *less* liabilities).

An *increase* in net assets leads to an increase in capital. A *decrease* in net assets leads to a decrease in capital.

Let me explain how increases or decreases in net assets occur.

- An **increase in net assets** occurs when shareholders inject more funds into the business in return for an increase in issued share capital, or when the business creates a gain in net assets.

- A **decrease in net assets occurs** when shareholders withdraw funds from the business, either through regular payments called **dividends**, or less frequently, when share capital is redeemed by the company, or when the business creates a loss in net assets.

Realised items and recognised items

When reporting the gains and losses incurred by the business, it is important to distinguish between items that have been **realised** and those items that are merely **recognised**.

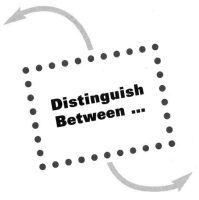

Realised items are profits and losses that have been substantiated by an actual financial transaction, such as selling stock for more than it was purchased for.

Distinguish Between ...

Recognised items are changes in the value of assets and liabilities that have not been realised, but which need to be allowed for by the user of the accounts. An example would be an increase in the value of a business's premises. This gain would only be realised when the property was sold.

2.9 REPORTING CHANGES IN OWNER'S EQUITY

Key Ideas

Equity and the balance sheet

Shareholder funds are represented in the balance sheet in different ways depending on how they have occurred.

The business has capital which has been contributed by its owners. It can also add to its capital internally by using profits in order to finance growth.

Amounts in respect of issued share capital are analysed into a **nominal value** and a **share premium**.

The **share premium** is the difference between the amount raised and the nominal value when new shares are raised.

Below is an example of a share premium.

Example

A share with a nominal value of £0.50 and issued at £0.75 would result in an increase in share capital of £0.50 and an increase in share premium of £0.25.

The profit and loss account

Realised profits and losses, net of dividend payments, are accumulated in the **profit and loss account**.

The business can use these retained profits to fund further growth without having to raise new finance from external sources. Other gains and losses are held in appropriately titled reserve accounts, e.g. the **revaluation account**.

Doctor Proctor outlines... **THE KEY FINANCIAL REPORTS**

To understand how shareholders' equity has changed, the following financial reports are required in the company's annual report and accounts:

- The **balance sheet** measures shareholders funds at a point in time.

- **Reconciliation of movements in shareholders' funds** records all changes to shareholders' equity between the current and the previous balance sheet dates.

- The **profit and loss account** provides details of realised trading revenues and expenses.

- The **statement of total recognised gains and losses** details recognised gains and losses that should be added to the realised profits and losses, such as property revaluations and foreign currency gains/losses.

2.9 REPORTING CHANGES IN OWNER'S EQUITY

Key Ideas 🔑

The main financial reports

At the end of Year 1 my Bright Ideas company had the following capital balances:

Example

	£000s
Share capital @ £1 per share	500
Share premium	250
Profit and loss account	800
	1,550

The following amounts arose during Year 2:

- The company raised £500,000 with the issue of shares at £2 each.
- The profit (realised) for the year was £250,000.
- Dividends were paid to shareholders amounting to £150,000.
- Property was revalued by £300,000.

Now see how these changes are reflected in the financial statements below.

Balance sheet – Year 1

	£000s
Share capital	500
Share premium	250
Profit and loss	800
Total	1,550

Reconciliation of movement in shareholder funds

	£000s
Profit for year	250
Dividends	−150
Share issue	500
Revaluation	300
Total increase	900

Balance sheet – Year 2

	£000s
Share capital	750
Share premium	500
Revaluation	300
Profit and loss	900
Total	2,450

New share issue (£500,000)

Dividends

Statement of total recognised gains and losses

	£000s
Profit	250
Revaluation	300
Total	550

Profit and loss account

	£000s
Profit	250
Dividends	150
Retained	100

Unrealised gains and losses – £300,000

2.10 THE PROFIT AND LOSS ACCOUNT

Key Ideas

What is revenue?

As we saw earlier, items only pass through the profit and loss account when they are realised. **Revenues** are the amounts received from customers arising from business activity.

Revenue is **realised** at the point when net assets (assets *less* liabilities) are increased. This may not coincide with when the customer actually pays.

Business is often conducted on the basis of an agreed credit period, and in accordance with the accrual concept, an asset in the form of a debtor is created at the time of supply. Alternative terms for revenue include **sales** or **turnover**.

Dr Proctor says:

'You Must Know This!'

The profit and loss account shows the sales revenues and expenses for a given period.

The basic structure is:

Revenue *less* Costs and Expenses = Profit

Here is a typical profit and loss account for my own company, Bright Ideas Plc.

Notes to the accounts give more information – for example, note 1 gives more information about turnover.

Doctor Proctor Bright Ideas Plc

Profit and Loss Account for the Year Ended 31 December 2001

	£000s
Turnover[1]	500
Cost of sales	200
Gross profit	300
Expenses:	
Distribution	75
Administration	150
Operating profit[2]	75
Net interest payable/receivable	10
Profit before tax	65
Tax[3]	20
Profit after tax	45
Dividends[4]	20
Profit retained	25

How profit was generated = revenue minus expenses

Appropriation of profit

2.10 THE PROFIT AND LOSS ACCOUNT

The essence of the profit and loss account is that it shows how business activity has created additional wealth for the business owners. It is therefore an important measure of financial performance and will be examined further in Section 5, **Ratio Analysis**.

The upper section of the profit and loss account shows how profit was generated.

- **Cost of sales** refers to the cost of goods or services supplied. For a retail business this would represent the purchase price of goods sold (the cost of goods *not* sold would be shown as stock in the balance sheet). For a manufacturing business, cost of sales includes wages and overheads incurred in the production process, as well as the cost of materials from suppliers.

- **Distribution expenses** include sales and marketing costs and the costs of physical distribution.

The lower section shows how profit has been appropriated between corporation tax paid to the Inland Revenue, dividends paid to shareholders and the retention of profits in the business.

Notes to the accounts provide more detailed analysis of certain items.

Doctor Proctor Bright Ideas Plc	
Profit and loss account	
For the year ended 31 December 2001	
	£000s
Turnover[1]	500
Cost of sales	200
Gross profit	300
Expenses:	
Distribution	75
Administration	150
Operating profit[2]	75
Net interest payable/receivable	10
Profit before tax	65
Tax[3]	20
Profit after tax	45
Dividends[4]	20
Profit retained	25

Doctor Proctor outlines... MORE ABOUT REALISATION OF INCOME AND EXPENSES

As we saw earlier, costs and expenses are **realised** when net assets are reduced. This occurs when a transaction diminishes net assets and there is no corresponding benefit to increase net assets.

For example, the cash purchase of stock for resale is **not** an expense, because a reduction in the asset 'cash' is offset by the increase in the asset 'stock'.

Likewise, paying an amount owed to a creditor is **not** an expense because the reduction in the asset 'cash' is offset by the reduction in liability.

However, a motor repair charged to a credit account **is** an expense because there is no offsetting increase in net assets for the incurred increase in liabilities.

2.11 THE CASH FLOW STATEMENT

Like the profit and loss account, the cash flow statement measures financial transactions for a specified period such as one year…Unlike the profit and loss account, the cash flow statement is concerned with *actual* cash receipts and payments and so does not follow the accruals concept.

It shows how the main categories of cash flow have changed the cash balance in particular periods.

Doctor Proctor outlines... TYPES OF CASH FLOW

The main categories of cash flow are:

1 **Net cash flow from operating activities.**
This consists of the receipts and payments arising from the company's business activities.

Doctor Proctor Calculates

My formula for net cash flow is:

Receipts from customers – Payments to suppliers and employees

(excluding payments for fixed assets)

2 **Returns on investment and servicing of finance**. This is calculated as:

Interest received – Interest paid

It shows to what extent debt finance is a burden on the business.

3 **Taxation**. This represents payments of corporation tax made during the accounting period.

4 **Capital expenditure** – i.e. the sum spent on fixed assets. Comparing this figure with the depreciation charge in the profit and loss account will give important pointers to future investment.

If the depreciation charge equates with the replacement spend required to maintain the average age and serviceability of fixed assets; then a higher spend would benefit the business and increase its capacity to generate profits.

A lower spend will have the opposite effect.

5 **Acquisitions.** This is the amount paid to acquire non-cash assets when buying other businesses.

6 **Equity dividends**. Payments to shareholders.

7 **Financing**. Amounts raised from, or repaid to, investors in the company. For example, repaying bank loans or raising fresh finance through an issue of shares.

2.11 THE CASH FLOW STATEMENT

Here is a typical cash flow statement for my company, Bright Ideas Plc.

Over time, a successful business is able to generate positive cash flows that can be distributed to shareholders. One of the key points to look for on the statement is the business's ability to generate cash inflows from operating activities.

Doctor Proctor Bright Ideas Plc

Cash Flow Statement
for the Year Ended 31 May 2002

	2002 £000s	2001 £000s
Net cash inflow from operating activities	1,400	900
Returns on investment and servicing of finance		
Interest paid	(200)	(200)
Capital expenditure		
Payment to acquire tangible fixed assets	(900)	(300)
Equity dividends paid	(350)	(250)
Net cash (outflow)/inflow before financing	(50)	150
Financing		
Bank loans	0	100
Finance lease repayments	(100)	(100)
Net cash outflow from financing	(100)	0
(Decrease)/increase in cash	(150)	150

Doctor Proctor outlines... EVALUATING CASH FLOW

From the above illustration you can see that whilst there has been a decrease in the overall cash balance of £150,000 during 2002, cash flows from operations increased by £500,000 compared to the previous year. The decrease in cash was due to:

1   an increased fixed asset spend which should benefit earnings capacity for future periods

2   an increase in dividends which directly increased cash in the hands of shareholders

3   the repayment of lease finance.

Although the cash flow statement is derived from information contained in the profit and loss account and balance sheet, the way it is presented highlights features that could otherwise be obscured.

2.12 REGULATION OF COMPANY ACCOUNTS

Key Ideas 🔑

Protecting the public interest

Dr Proctor says:
'You Must Know This!'

One of the key aims of regulating business activity is to safeguard the public interest. In many companies the shareholders have little involvement in the day-to-day running of the business. To ensure consistent high quality of financial reporting, there must be a regulatory framework.

Doctor Proctor outlines... THE MAIN FORMS OF FINANCIAL REGULATION

The main forms of regulation are:

1

The Companies Acts

The minimum legal requirements are contained in the Companies Acts.

These require the publication of an annual report to shareholders.

2

FRSs and SSAPs

The financial reports contained in the annual report are also subject to **Financial Reporting Standards (FRSs)** and the older **Statements of Standard Accounting Practice (SSAPs)** which are now gradually being replaced.

FRSs are issued by the **Accounting Standards Board** which reports to the independent **Financial Reporting Council** which represents accountants and users of accounts. Accounting standards augment the legal requirements with what is considered best accounting practice on numerous technical issues. These range from the basic concepts of accounting to detailed guidance on how to calculate specific items such as fixed asset depreciation.

3

The Listing Rules

Companies listed on the London Stock Exchange must also comply with the requirements on reporting laid down in **The Listing Rules**. These require six-monthly reporting and describe how financial results and trading updates should be communicated to ensure a fair and efficient market for the buying and selling of shares. The aim is that all investors should have access to the same information at the same time.

2.12 REGULATION OF COMPANY ACCOUNTS

Key Ideas

Reporting rules

Every company must present an annual report to shareholders and submit a copy to Companies House. This must be done within 10 months of the year-end for a private limited company, and within 7 months of the year-end in the case of a plc.

The regulations on the presentation of annual reports are listed opposite.

1 **Content**. The annual report must include a directors' report, auditors' report, profit and loss account, balance sheet, cash flow statement, statement of total gains and losses and various notes to the accounts.

2 **Format**. Forms of presentation are prescribed for the various financial reports. Some minor variations are allowed if users' understanding is improved as a result.

3 **Basis of valuation of assets and liabilities**. The rules permit either historical cost or an alternative based on current costs.

Doctor Proctor outlines... HOW THE REGULATIONS* ARE POLICED

Shareholders appoint **auditors** to assess whether the accounts give a 'true and fair' view of the company's position. Auditors are required to review the business's accounting records, current operations and future prospects. In addition the **Financial Reporting Review Panel** checks annual reports for compliance with legislation and FRSs. The diagram on the right shows how the various regulations (shown down the centre of the diagram) are created by the various responsible bodies.

* Shown across the centre of the diagram

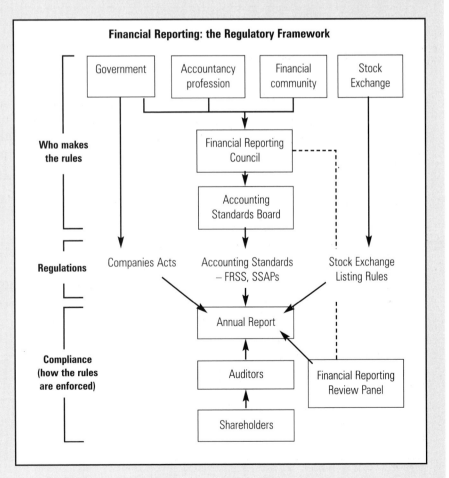

2.13 REPORTING FINANCIAL PERFORMANCE

Key Ideas 🔑

Accounts for shareholders

The profit and loss account aims to show how the company's business activities have added to shareholder wealth. But it can also provide useful further information – for example, about the profitability of different areas of company activity.

If the company is engaged in more than one type of business, or more than one geographical market, a **segmental analysis** is required, with each business or geographical area being considered as a separate segment.

Also, if the company has acquired or terminated business activities, or has experienced some other unusual circumstance, this will need to be clearly highlighted.

Doctor Proctor outlines... SEGMENTAL ANALYSIS

Companies need to analyse the turnover, operating profit and net assets of the business according to relevant business **segments**.

These segments may be:

- different **types of business**, e.g. a leisure company may distinguish between health clubs and night clubs

- different **geographical areas**, e.g. an engineering company may report separately on operations in the UK, Europe, USA and other regions.

Example

Notes to the accounts: segmental analysis

	Turnover £000s	Operating profit £000s	Net assets £000s
Health clubs	1,500	300	1,800
Night clubs	1,250	50	2,000
Total	**2,750**	**350**	**3,800**

Geographical analysis of turnover and profit should be based on the location of business operations (i.e. place of origin).

Where businesses export into other areas, a geographical analysis of turnover by destination is also required.

2.13 REPORTING FINANCIAL PERFORMANCE

Key Ideas

Reporting business changes

In some cases it may be difficult to make meaningful comparison of performance between different periods.

For example, accounting standards require further information to be included where:

1. the company has acquired new businesses, or sold or terminated previous activities
2. the company has experienced an **exceptional item**, i.e. an event or factor that is either unusual in itself, or is of an unusual size or scale.

Where business acquisitions or terminations have taken place, turnover, cost of sales, expenses and operating profit must be analysed between the relevant parts of the business.

Turnover and profit must be analysed in the profit and loss account. The other items are usually analysed in notes to the accounts.

Example

The table on the right shows how 'unusual circumstances' might appear in a set of accounts.

What does the illustration tell you about the relative profitability of the business's continuing and discontinued activities? What does it imply for the future?

		£000s
Turnover	**Continuing operations**	5,000
	Acquisitions	2,000
		7,000
Discontinued operations		500
		7,500
Cost of sales		4,000
Gross profit	(Analysed in a supporting 'note')	3,500
Distribution costs		1,000
Administration expenses		1,000
Operating profit	**Continuing operations**	1,250
	Acquisitions	500
		1,750
	Discontinued operations	– 250
		1,500

2.13 REPORTING FINANCIAL PERFORMANCE

'Exceptional items' in a company's accounts must be reported in accordance with the rules, or they may give a misleading picture of the business's overall financial performance.

The guidelines for reporting exceptional items are explained below.

Doctor Proctor outlines... REPORTING EXCEPTIONAL ITEMS

An item is **exceptional** if:

- it does not usually occur, e.g. redundancy payments on closing down a factory

- it is unusually large, e.g. a major customer defaults on a debt to the company.

Exceptional items are either shown in the profit and loss account or are detailed in notes to the accounts.

By extracting the exceptional item it is possible to form a more accurate view of the underlying trend in financial performance.

In the example, analysis shows that profits only increased in 2002 due to the exceptional item. As you can see, this puts a completely different complexion on the company's financial performance.

Example

ABC company highlighted a profit on the sale of a factory building in its accounts for 2002.

Below is an extract from the profit and loss account:

	2002	2001
	£000s	*£000s*
Operating profit	1,000	1,500
Exceptional item:		
Profit on sale of fixed asset	1,000	0
Profit before interest	2,000	1,500

Fixed assets

Peach Ltd purchased a forklift truck for £9,000 to be used in the firm's stores. The company's depreciation policy is to assume that this type of asset will be in use for 5 years, and at the end of this time there would be no residual value.

1 Why would a forklift truck be considered a fixed asset?
2 Calculate the annual depreciation charge.
3 What will be the net book value after 1 year and 4 years?

Current assets

1 Here are assets owned by a motor garage:

   * Workshop machinery: £5,000
   * A pile of invoices for workshop repairs that have not yet been paid by customers: £3,000
   * Motor parts: £3,000
   * Cash at bank: £1,500
   * Motor cars in the showroom: £50,000
   * Garage premises: £100,000.

   Identify which items are current assets.

2 Calculate the value for each of the following categories of current asset:

   * Stocks
   * Debtors
   * Cash.

3 For any assets remaining, explain why they are not current assets.

Liabilities

1 Taking an annual report for a limited company, find the notes to the accounts that explain the make-up of 'creditors due within one year' and 'creditors due after one year'.
2 Why do you think the accounts distinguish between the two categories?
3 What type of liability tends to predominate in each category?

Accounting concepts

1 What are the four main accounting concepts?
2 Why might the 'going concern' concept undermine the normal valuation of assets?
3 State an appropriate valuation for the following items:

   * Stock: category A cost £5,000 and can be sold for £7,000; category B cost £2,000 and can be sold for £1,500.
   * Debtors: an invoice for £9,000 is considered 99% certain of being paid; for an old invoice of £1,000 the customer can no longer be contacted.
   * Trade creditor: goods were purchased for £5,000 on credit terms and have yet to be paid.

Owner's capital

Explain the differences between the following items:

1 Joan Smith v. Joan Smith Ltd
2 Ltd v. Plc
3 Ordinary shares v. preference shares
4 Authorised share capital v. issued share capital.

Third-party finance

1 Categorise the different forms of third-party finance according to time periods: short, medium and long.
2 Which types of finance are tied to specific assets?

The balance sheet

1 If total assets = £50,000 and total equity provided by shareholders = £35,000, what is the value of liabilities?
2 Following the example on page 26, construct a balance sheet from the following:

Continued on page 40

Continued from page 39:

- Tangible fixed assets: £40,000
- Cash: £5,000
- Creditors due after more than one year: £15,000
- Share capital: £10,000
- Retained profits: £25,000
- Creditors due within one year: £18,000
- Debtors: £8,000.

Reporting changes in owner's equity

1 Distinguish between 'realised' and 'recognised' gains to shareholders' equity.

2 Using the headings of 'realised', 'recognised' and 'other changes', categorise the following changes to the capital balance:

- Revalue a property from £50,000 to £60,000.
- Issue new shares £10,000.
- Pay a dividend to shareholders of £5,000.
- Sell goods to customers for £15,000 that had originally cost £8,000.
- Pay royalties to the designer of the firm's products £1,000.

3 In which financial report will the 'realised' profits and losses be shown?

The profit and loss account

Referring to Doctor Proctor's Bright Ideas Ltd profit and loss account (page 30), describe how the following terms are calculated:

1 Gross profit
2 Operating profit
3 Profit retained.

The cash flow statement

1 The cash flow statement and the profit and loss account are similar in that they each describe how particular values in the balance sheet have changed over a specified period. What are the two values in question?

2 What accounting concept differentiates the two financial reports?

Regulation of company accounts

As part of the regulatory framework for financial reporting, explain the role of the following:

1 Government
2 Financial Reporting Council
3 Auditors

Reporting financial performance

1 Explain what is meant by the term 'segmental analysis'.

2 Why might segmental analysis be useful to users of accounts?

3 Explain what is meant by the term 'exceptional items'.

4 Why should exceptional items be highlighted?

5 What items of the profit and loss account must be analysed if acquisitions or terminations have been made?

6 Why do you think this information is valuable?

UNIT 3

FINANCIAL MANAGEMENT

Topics covered in this unit

3.1 Managing Cashflow
How a company can control the amount of cash that it holds.

3.2 Investment Appraisal
A commonly used approach to weighing up the return on investments.

3.3 Investment Appraisal: Discounted Cash Flow
How to value future returns on investment in terms of what these returns would be worth today.

3.4 Investment Appraisal: Net Present Value
How to calculate the present value of a future cash flow.

3.5 Investment Appraisal: Accounting Rate of Return
How the profits from a business investment can be compared with the capital sum invested.

Questions

Unit 3 describes the nature of cash flow and financial management in an organisation.

3.1 MANAGING CASHFLOW

Key Ideas

Active cash management

Cash management is concerned with the efficient use of financial resources.

Without **active management**, financial resources are either wasted or are uneconomically tied up in the form of other assets. A profitable company is not necessarily a **cash-rich** one.

Remember that profit is calculated according to the **accruals concep**t (see page 16).

A company may have paid for expensive fixed assets, stocks and other resources, but only those that can be matched to revenues will have been deducted in the profit and loss account.

So a company may be profitable, but if the business does not have the cash to satisfy financial obligations to employees and suppliers, its survival may be at risk.

Successful cash flow management is all about having enough (but not too much) cash available when the business needs it.

To avoid liquidity problems, businesses need to follow the principles described here.

1 Avoid tying up too many funds in fixed assets

Most liquidity problems are the result of investment in working capital, but funds can also be unnecessarily tied up in fixed assets.

The purchase of fixed assets must involve the best use of funds, and to this end, should be the subject of formal capital expenditure authorisation procedures.

Appraisal techniques (see **Sections 3.2–3.5**) should consider the costs and benefits of investment versus alternatives such as short-term hire.

Unlike investment in working capital, expenditure on fixed assets is often discretionary, and authorisation is usually the sole prerogative of senior management.

2 Monitor stock levels

Stocks in the form of raw materials or finished goods often represent a significant investment. Good stock control minimises the risk of holding either too much or too little stock.

The business needs enough stock to satisfy customer demands in terms of range and delivery lead times, but it also needs to control the costs of buying and storing materials, including handling, insurance and clerical expenses.

High stock levels also increase the risk of obsolescence, deterioration and theft. The business should aim for high stock turnover with systematic ordering in line with economic batch quantities.

3.1 MANAGING CASHFLOW

Key Ideas

Cash management: the payment side

Clearly it is better for a business to have cash in its own bank account than in the hands of its suppliers.

Many businesses aim to maximise trade credit because it is free of finance charges, and so only pay suppliers when chased. However, firms who take a more ethical, long-term view believe that paying within agreed credit terms helps build better trading relationships.

Managing debtor balances

Outstanding debtor balances in excess of the credit terms agreed with customers are an unnecessary and expensive drain on cash resources. As well as costing money to finance, old debts become difficult to collect.

Without effective credit control, firms risk adding to bad debts with continuing supplies. They need to check the financial status of new customers and chase up customers as soon as payment is late.

Managing debts

In the case of sources of finance, a business should manage its **portfolio of debt** to ensure that redemption dates correspond with periods when the company is likely to generate surplus operating cash flow or when refinancing is considered beneficial.

Doctor Proctor outlines... INVESTING EXCESS CASH BALANCES

When a business has excess cash balances, its financial managers need to invest it in accordance with these three principles.

Most business investments tend to be conservative and are biased towards bank deposits, government bonds and money-market deposits.

1

Safety of sum invested
Generally the risk should be very low

2

Duration
The investment must be capable of being liquidated quickly according to business need

3

Financial return
This needs to be as large as possible, consistent with the need for safety

3.2 INVESTMENT APPRAISAL

Key Ideas

What is an 'investment'?

The development and growth of a business usually takes place in a series of separate steps or projects. These can range from the purchase of an additional delivery van to the complete take-over of another business.

These projects are **investments** because they involve adding to or replacing some of the operating assets of the business.

Investment objectives

The aim of an investment may be to:

1. expand capacity
2. replace existing assets that are no longer economical to use, or are technologically obsolete
3. comply with health and safety regulations.

The decision whether or not to invest in a particular project should be based on a financial appraisal to check that benefits outweigh costs, and that the return is sufficient to meet the organisation's objectives.

The main criteria for appraising an investment are discussed below.

Doctor Proctor outlines... APPRAISING AN INVESTMENT

A particular feature of most investment situations is that an outflow of cash *today* is to be measured against benefits to be received *in the future*, sometimes over many years.

This raises a number of issues:

1. Because the future is never predictable, estimates of future revenues and costs are likely to be less accurate the further into the future we look.

2. Factors that can affect the project's success include:

   - changes in government and in the law

   - fluctuating economic conditions such as interest rates, exchange rates and unemployment

   - changing market conditions such as competition and consumer trends.

3. Measured in cash terms, benefits in the future are not as valuable as benefits received today. This 'time value' of money is illustrated by the fact that the business will incur interest charges on debt used to finance the project.

Investments that businesses make today are repaid in future benefits – but the further into the future we look, the less certain we can be in measuring the likely returns.

3.2 INVESTMENT APPRAISAL

The 'planning horizon'

new power station is likely to require at least a 10-year planning horizon; an advertising campaign may look just 1 or 2 years ahead.

There are a number of possible ways to appraise an investment opportunity. A common approach is to set a realistic **planning horizon** beyond which benefits are not taken into account.

This planning horizon will depend on the nature of the project. For example, the appraisal of a

Long-term investment   **Short-term investment**

Doctor Proctor outlines... THE PAYBACK PERIOD

A commonly used investment appraisal technique is the **payback method**.

The **payback period** is the time required for a project to repay the initial investment.

The calculation is based on cash flows and not on profits.

The annual cash flows are cumulated and the payback period is reached when the cumulative cash flow reaches zero.

Doctor Proctor Calculates

Use this formula for calculating the payback period:

$$\text{Years with negative cumulative cash flow} + \frac{\text{Deficit remaining}}{\text{Cash flow in relevant year}} \times 12 \text{ months}$$

Example

	Year	Project cash flow £	Cumulative cash flow £
Investment in fixed assets	0	− 45,000	− 45,000
Net inflows of cash	1	15,000	− 30,000
	2	25,000	− 5,000
	3	20,000	15,000

In the illustration on the left, payback is reached between the end of Year 2 and the end of Year 3.

So, in the example given in the chart:

Payback =

$$2 \text{ years} + 12 \text{ months} \times \frac{£5,000}{£20,000}$$

= 2 years 3 months

The project with the shortest payback period is the best investment proposition, as the shorter time scale reduces the risk of unforeseen circumstances.

3.3 INVESTMENT APPRAISAL: DISCOUNTED CASH FLOW

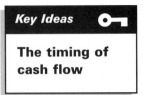

Key Ideas

The timing of cash flow

A second technique for appraising an investment is to use discounted cash flow.

The **discounted cash flow approach** is a way of valuing the future returns on investment by assessing the value of these returns in terms of their present value. It places emphasis on the cost of funds tied up in a project by considering the **timing** of cash flows.

For example, we all instinctively know that £1 in the hand today is worth more than a promise of £1 in the future. This is because:

- there is always a risk that unforeseen circumstances will prevent you receiving the amount you have been promised
- inflation may lower the real value of money
- the money cannot be put to constructive use in the meantime. The delay in payment therefore incurs an **opportunity cost**.

This 'time value' of money is often represented by a composite annual percentage rate. Bank deposit rates, for example, often include amounts to cover the elements described above.

Let's take a look at the principle of discounted cash flow.

Example

Discounted cash flow works on the same principles as compound interest.

Consider a sum of £100 that is invested in a savings account that yields interest at 10% per annum. Assuming that the interest is left in the account at the end of each year, the savings account balance for the next four years will be:

Year	10% interest	Balance £
0	–	100.00
1	10.00	110.00
2	11.00	121.00
3	12.10	133.10
4	13.31	146.41

What does this mean in terms of net present value?

Using an interest rate of 10%:

- £110.00 in 1 year's time is worth £100.00 today.
- £146.41 in 4 years' time is worth £100.00 today.

By reducing all future cash flows to a common measure in this way, comparisons can be made between projects.

3.4 INVESTMENT APPRAISAL: NET PRESENT VALUE

Dr Proctor says:
'You Must Know This!'

The total of all cash flows restated in today's money terms is called the **net present value (NPV)**.

Net present value is based on actual cash flows. These will include:

Inflows

- Sales revenues, phased according to when they will actually be received
- Sales proceeds from the disposal of fixed assets at the conclusion of a project
- Release of amounts invested in stocks at the end of a project
- Government grants.

Outflows

- Investment in fixed assets
- Creation of a working stock balance
- Operating costs, including material, labour and expenses.

Doctor Proctor outlines... CALCULATING THE NPV OF A FUTURE CASH FLOW

The NPV of a future cash flow is found by multiplying it by a **discount factor**.

The size of the factor depends on the discount rate used (cost of capital) and the number of years involved.

The easiest way of finding a discount factor is to look it up in an **NPV table** (below). This can save a lot of time and effort.

For example, the table shows that cash in 4 years' time discounted at 10% should be multiplied by a factor of 0.6830.

						Interest Rate						
Year	**5%**	**6%**	**7%**	**8%**	**9%**	**10%**	**11%**	**12%**	**13%**	**14%**	**15%**	**20%**
1	0.9524	0.9434	0.9346	0.9259	0.9174	0.9091	0.9009	0.8929	0.8850	0.8772	0.8698	0.8333
2	0.9070	0.8900	0.8734	0.8793	0.8417	0.8264	0.8116	0.7972	0.7831	0.7695	0.7561	0.6944
3	0.8638	0.8396	0.8163	0.7938	0.7722	0.7513	0.7312	0.7118	0.6931	0.6750	0.6575	0.5787
4	0.8277	0.7921	0.7629	0.7350	0.7084	0.6830	0.6587	0.6355	0.6133	0.5921	0.5718	0.4823
5	0.7835	0.7473	0.7130	0.6806	0.6499	0.6209	0.5935	0.5674	0.5428	0.5194	0.4972	0.4019
6	07462	0.7050	0.6663	0.6302	0.5963	0.5645	0.5346	0.5066	0.4803	0.4556	0.4323	0.3349
7	0.7107	0.6651	0.6227	0.5835	0.5470	0.5132	0.4817	0.4523	0.4251	0.3996	0.3759	0.2791
8	0.6768	0.6274	0.5820	0.5403	0.5019	0.4665	0.4339	0.4039	0.3762	0.3506	0.3269	0.2326
9	0.6446	0.5919	0.5439	0.5002	0.4604	0.4241	0.3909	0.3606	0.3329	0.3075	0.2843	0.1938

3.4 INVESTMENT APPRAISAL: NET PRESENT VALUE

Key Ideas 🔑

Calculating the Discount Factor

When calculating Net Present Value, it is also possible to calculate the discount factor without having to rely on NPV tables. The method of calculation is shown on the right.

Doctor Proctor Calculates

NPV discount factor =

$$\frac{1}{(1 + r)^n}$$

where:

r = discount rate

n = number of years

For example, cash received in 4 years' time to be discounted at 10% is calculated as follows:

$$\text{NPV discount factor} = \frac{1}{(1 + 0.1)^4} = \mathbf{0.6830}$$

Example

Now let me show you how discount factors are used to calculate NPV.

	Year	Cash flow	10% factor discount	Net present value
		£		£
Investment in fixed assets	0	− 45,000	1.000	− 45,000
	1	15,000	0.909	13,635
	2	25,000	0.826	20,650
	3	20,000	0.751	15,020
Total		**15,000**		**4,305**

The net present value here is positive: £4,305. This indicates that the project earns a rate in excess of the firm's 10% cost of capital.

As an individual project, this investment would be given the go-ahead. Where a number of projects are competing for the financial resources of a company, the project chosen would be the one with the highest NPV.

3.5 INVESTMENT APPRAISAL: ACCOUNTING RATE OF RETURN

Key Ideas

Comparing profit with capital invested

Doctor Proctor Calculates

$$ARR = \frac{\text{Average annual profits}}{\text{Average capital employed}} \times 100\%$$

A third investment appraisal technique is the accounting rate of return (ARR).

Accounting profit is routinely used to measure business performance, so it makes sense to use it as a basis for appraising investment projects too.

The accounting rate of return compares **profits** (calculated according to the accounting policies of the business) with the **capital** invested in the project.

Just as a personal investor might compare interest rates between building societies, a business will choose the project with the highest accounting rate of return.

Here's an example of ARR, using the same project as on page 48. But note that the figures have been converted from cash flows to accounting profit by depreciating the original investment over the next 4 years.

Example

	Year	Project cash flow	Capitalise asset and depreciate	Project profit
		£	£	£
Investment in fixed assets	0	− 45,000	45,000	
Net inflows of cash	1	15,000	− 15,000	0
	2	25,000	− 15,000	10,000
	3	20,000	− 15,000	5,000

$$\text{Average profit per annum} = \frac{£0 + £10,000 + £5,000}{3}$$

$$= £5,000$$

Continued on page 50

3.5 INVESTMENT APPRAISAL: ACCOUNTING RATE OF RETURN

Discounted cash flow is generally considered the most sophisticated of the investment appraisal techniques. However, the payback period method, despite its shortcomings, is widely used because it is the simplest of the techniques to calculate and to evaluate.

In practice many firms use more than one method and require minimum criteria to be met for each – for example, payback within 3 years and positive NPV before 5 years.

Example (cont'd)

Average capital employed is calculated by taking a simple average between the capital invested at the start of a project and the balance at the end of it (nil residue value in this case).

$$\text{Average capital employed} = \frac{£45,000}{2} = £22,500$$

Now you can work out the ARR.

$$\text{Accounting rate of return} = \frac{£5,000}{£22,500} \times 100\% = 22.2\%$$

Project rates of return are compared with the business's cost of capital (e.g. cost of borrowing) before commencing.

Where choices have to be made between competing projects, the project with the highest ARR is preferred.

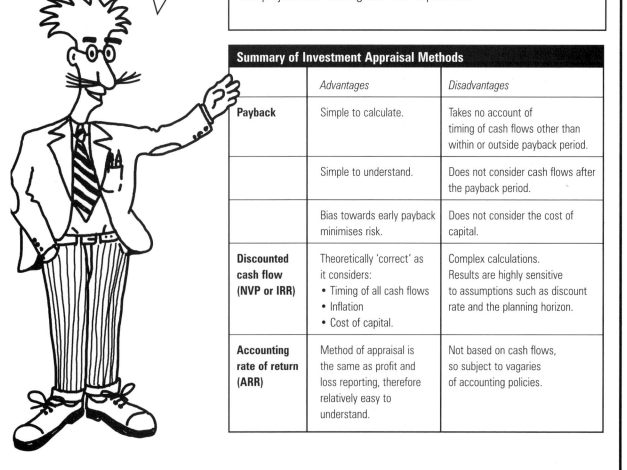

Summary of Investment Appraisal Methods

	Advantages	Disadvantages
Payback	Simple to calculate.	Takes no account of timing of cash flows other than within or outside payback period.
	Simple to understand.	Does not consider cash flows after the payback period.
	Bias towards early payback minimises risk.	Does not consider the cost of capital.
Discounted cash flow (NVP or IRR)	Theoretically 'correct' as it considers: • Timing of all cash flows • Inflation • Cost of capital.	Complex calculations. Results are highly sensitive to assumptions such as discount rate and the planning horizon.
Accounting rate of return (ARR)	Method of appraisal is the same as profit and loss reporting, therefore relatively easy to understand.	Not based on cash flows, so subject to vagaries of accounting policies.

QUESTIONS

Investment appraisal

Identify whether the following items are one-off or recurring; and whether they are inflows or outflows of cash:

- sales revenue
- shopfloor wages
- purchase of fixed assets
- purchase of stocks for production
- selling fixed assets at end of project
- tax payable on profits
- initial product marketing
- royalties paid to product designer.

Supercolour Printers Ltd

Supercolour Printers Ltd currently has to turn work down because it has insufficient print capacity. A new printing press would cost £400,000, but would enable £500,000-worth of additional work each year to be processed. Annual running costs will be 2 operatives at £25,000 each and materials amounting to £100,000.

1   Calculate the payback period.
2   Calculate the net book value, assuming the company' policy is to discount 4 years of cash flows at 20% per annum.
3   Calculate the accounting rate of return, assuming the printing press is depreciated over 4 years.

Supercolour printers has another investment opportunity. Currently, the work of cutting out card from printed sheets has to be done out-of-house. To do the work in-house requires a die-cutting machine that would cost £300,000. Although the machine would cost £100,000 a year to run, it would erase the annual cutting charges of £325,000.

4   Calculate the payback period.
5   Calculate the net book value based on a 20% discount rate.
6   Calculate the accounting rate of return.
7   Unfortunately, the company does not have sufficient financing facilities to fund both the printing press and the die-cutting machine. Which investment opportunity should the company pursue, based on the numbers presented here?

Multiple choice questions

Identify the correct statement from the following:

1   'Payback period' refers to:

   a)   The period up to the point at which a project becomes profitable
   b)   The time taken for the initial investment in a project to be repaid with subsequent cash inflows
   c)   The time allowed before the bank must be repaid.

2   'Net present value' refers to:

   a)   All future cash flows being compounded at an appropriate rate of return into the future.
   b)   For a given project, the present value of all cash inflows *less* the present value of all cash outflows.
   c)   Present cash resources less future net receipts of cash.

3   The most important criterion for the investment of temporary surplus funds is:

   a)   high rate of return
   b)   low risk
   c)   long investment period.

4   The discount factor used in calculating present values derives directly from:

   a)   current inflation rates
   b)   the rate of return expected by the firm's investors
   c)   bank base rates.

5   Financial appraisal techniques are less appropriate for:

   a)   expenditure to comply with health and safety regulations
   b)   projects for expansion
   c)   projects for closing down a business.

Topics covered in this unit

This unit explains the importance of budgeting and forecasting as planning and control tools for managers.

4.1 Introducing Budgets and Forecasts
The difference between a budget and a forecast; the importance of budgeting as a financial and management tool.

4.2 Preparing a Budget
Putting together the building blocks' of a budget.

4.3 Budget Variances
Identifying the gap between what the budget sets out to achieve and what is actually achieved.

4.4 The Cash Flow Forecast
Using the cash flow forecast to identify how cash is used in a business and to allow for cash inflows and outflows.

Questions

4.1 INTRODUCING BUDGETS AND FORECASTS

Budgets and forecasts are both concerned with future financial performance, but there is an important difference between them.

A **forecast** is an estimate based on how the business is currently run (*passive*).

Distinguish between ...

A **budget** is about formulating plans and making decisions to achieve a financial target (*active*).

Doctor Proctor outlines... THE BUDGETING PROCESS

The budget process aims to provide:

- a coherent plan so that all parts of the business are working towards a common goal

- a control tool and a catalyst for management action if actual performance varies from planned performance.

The budget is made up of a set of statements that set out the planned financial performance of the business, from individual departments to a total business budget for the profit and loss account and balance sheet.

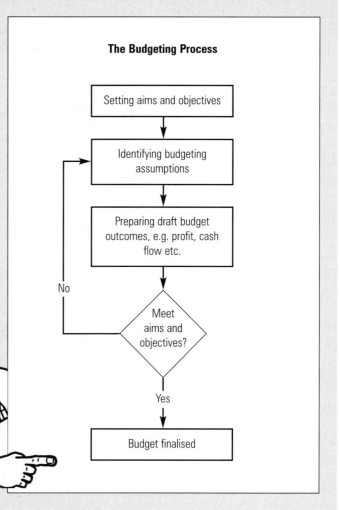

The Budgeting Process

Setting aims and objectives

↓

Identifying budgeting assumptions

↓

Preparing draft budget outcomes, e.g. profit, cash flow etc.

↓

Meet aims and objectives? — No

↓ Yes

Budget finalised

4.1 INTRODUCING BUDGETS AND FORECASTS

Key Ideas

Budgeting: advantages and disadvantages

Every organisation needs to create and then monitor its budget. The budget enables clear planning to take place coupled with ongoing checks on performance.

BUDGETING Advantages

1 Forces busy managers to think about the future and to formulate goals and strategies.

2 Exposes strategies and policies that will fail to deliver. It is better to fail on paper than in reality.

3 Enforces consistency. Every department works towards the same goals with the same set of assumptions regarding sales volumes, selling prices, cost levels, etc.

4 Allows effective performance measurement. It is possible to compare actual performance (what happens in reality) with budgeted performance (what was planned to happen).

5 A communication and motivational tool. The budget process sets out clear business objectives and who is responsible for achieving them.

BUDGETING Disadvantages

1 Can reduce emphasis on important long-term planning. A detailed annual budget seems real and immediate and hence emphasises the short term.

2 Time-consuming.

3 Budgets are often inflexible. In the real world, circumstances change. However, businesses may seek to stick to their original budget plans because managers are reluctant to give up the control that the budget appears to give them.

4.2 PREPARING A BUDGET

Key Ideas 🔑

Budgeting: the 'building block' approach

A budget needs to be constructed using a 'building block' approach

Step 1: The foundations are laid.

- Senior management set the long-term objectives and strategies, the planning horizon, etc.

- Environmental factors are analysed including economic, social, technological and regulatory factors.

- Market conditions are forecast in order to assess production costs, cost of supplies, labour and finance.

Long-term strategy	Long-term strategy	Long-term strategy

Step 2: The structure is developed.

- Sales volumes and prices are forecast. Business activity is quantified, required resources are evaluated.

- Production volumes are estimated.

- Production resources such as raw materials, personnel, fixed assets and production overheads are costed.

- Direct support functions (e.g. factory maintenance, stores and distribution) are added, followed by indirect support functions such as personnel, sales and finance.

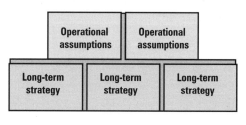

Step 3: Cost centre budgets are finalised.

The budgeting process results in budgets being developed for each area of business activity.

The money values used are often linked to quantities (units, weights and other measures) to ensure consistency across the various functions. They also provide relevance to operational activity and so make it easy to monitor ongoing performance of a function.

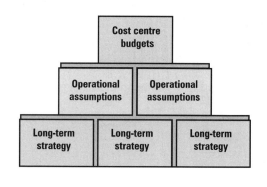

4.2 PREPARING A BUDGET

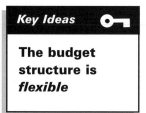

Key Ideas

The budget structure is *flexible*

The exact format of a budget depends on the business needs – for example, the structure of the firm and its operational processes. It is, however, usual for each budget to be analysed by time period, e.g. by week or by month.

For example, a sales budget could be analysed by type of supply and/or by sales region:

Regional Sales Budget			
	April	**May**	**June**
	£000s	*£000s*	*£000s*
UK	500	600	550
USA	250	300	350
Asia	100	150	200
Totals	**850**	**1,050**	**1,100**

In order for a budget to be motivating for employees and to foster a sense of ownership, as many people as possible need to be involved in the budgeting process.

Departmental or team budgets also need to be seen as being realistic and attainable – i.e. not too easy or too difficult to achieve.

If the budget is merely a senior management 'wish list', the exercise will be a waste of time at best. At worst it will be misleading and will fail to deliver its stated objectives.

Doctor Proctor outlines... LIMITING FACTORS

During budget preparation, it is important to ensure that departmental budgets are consistent on a period-by-period basis, and to identify any **limiting factors** that will restrict business volume – for example, lack of skilled workers, machine capacity or funding to finance working capital. For many businesses the limiting factor will be the level of sales.

An example of an exercise to identify and correct a limiting factor is give on page 58.

The importance of planning
Where possible, the effects of the limiting factor should be minimised by careful planning. For example, if production of non-perishable goods cannot keep up with sales during a particular month, it will be necessary to build up stocks during the preceding months.

4.2 PREPARING A BUDGET

Example

A furniture manufacturer has production capacity of 1,000 tables a month. The manufacturer aims to have a stock of 250 tables at any time.

Sales of tables are forecast to be 500 in September and October, 750 in November, 1,000 in December, and 1,500 in January.

A production budget is prepared to cover this five-month period.

The problem is that in January, sales will exceed production capacity by 500 tables. By working back from January it is possible to find the nearest months that will have sufficient excess production capacity to build up stocks in readiness for the January sales.

Many budgets are constructed using financial details such as the cash received and spent by a business. But other budgets use non-financial information, for example, physical units of production in a production budget and employee hours in a labour budget.

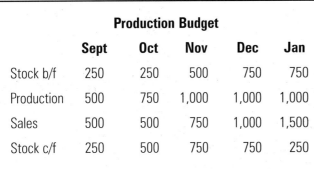

Production Budget

	Sept	Oct	Nov	Dec	Jan
Stock b/f	250	250	500	750	750
Production	500	750	1,000	1,000	1,000
Sales	500	500	750	1,000	1,500
Stock c/f	250	500	750	750	250

As December's figure for maximum production is matched by sales, October and November are the last months in which stocks can be built up before the January peak period. To increase stocks in September would unnecessarily increase the period of investment in high stocks.

4.3 BUDGET VARIANCES

Key Ideas 🔑

Identifying and controlling variances

A budget is more than a simple forecast. It provides a **benchmark** against which actual performance can be measured. Budgetary control requires the calculation of the variance between actual and budget.

A *variance* is a difference between what actually happens and what is budgeted to happen.

As you can see in the table below, the variance may be **favourable** or **adverse**.

	Actual greater than budget	Actual lower than budget
Sales/Turnover/Income	Favourable	Adverse
Costs/Expenses	Adverse	Favourable

Doctor Proctor outlines... VARIANCE ANALYSIS

Variance analysis is a catalyst for management action.

Following the approach known as **management by exception**, managers can be alerted to significant variances, investigate their causes and take prompt corrective action. The aim is to focus on a small number of 'exceptional' cases (where action is needed) rather than attempting to monitor every case in detail.

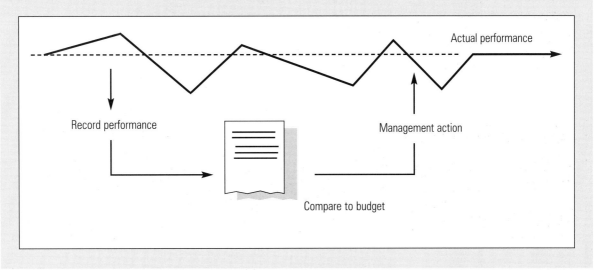

4.3 BUDGET VARIANCES

The table below shows an annual departmental budget for my company, Bright Ideas Plc.

This has been used to compare with actual performance in the budget report below. Which of the variances are favourable and which are adverse?

Doctor Proctor Bright Ideas Plc

Annual departmental budget (£000s)

	Total	Jan	Feb	Mar	Apr	May	June	July	Aug	Sept	Oct	Nov	Dec
Salaries	**127.0**	10.0	10.0	10.0	10.0	10.0	10.0	11.0	11.0	11.0	11.0	11.0	12.0
Travel	**37.0**	1.5	1.5	2.0	2.0	3.0	5.0	4.0	4.0	6.0	4.0	2.5	1.5
Stationery	**34.0**	2.0	2.0	2.0	2.0	2.5	2.5	2.5	2.5	2.5	2.5	8.0	3.0

Doctor Proctor Bright Ideas Plc

Monthly budget report

	June			Year to date		
	Actual	Budget	Variance	Actual	Budget	Variance
Salaries	10.2	10.0	(0.2)	61.8	60.0	(1.8)
Travel	4.1	5.0	0.9	14.5	15.0	0.5
Stationery	1.9	2.5	0.6	12.9	13.0	0.1

4.3 BUDGET VARIANCES

Key Ideas 🔑

Flexibility in budgeting

Budgets are not updated to take account of minor variances. This would undermine the control objectives of the process.

If a manager overspends on an item in one month, the situation can be rectified in the next.

However, the budget must remain relevant and should not discriminate between things that are within management control and those that are not.

For example, if the sales force achieves higher sales than expected, other departments will need to provide increased levels of goods or services as well.

Doctor Proctor outlines... FLEXING THE BUDGET

In order to allow for items that vary with changes in volumes, budgets need to be **flexed**.

Adjustments are not made merely because items are more expensive than was forecast, and nor are they made to cost headings that should remain fixed whatever the sales volume.

> Let me show you an example of what a flexed budget might look like for a garage services department.

Example

In a particular month, the number of hours charged to customers has increased by 10%.

Service department expenses	Fixed/ variable	Original budget	Flexed budget	Change %
		£	£	
Rent of workshop	Fixed	10,000	10,000	0.0
Mechanics wages	Variable	20,000	22,000	10.0
Depreciation of equipment	Fixed	2,000	2,000	0.0
		32,000	**34,000**	

Variances will be calculated with reference to the 'revised' or 'flexed' budget.

4.4 THE CASH FLOW FORECAST

Here's an example of a cash flow forecast for my company, Bright Ideas Plc.

The cash flow forecast sets out a business's forecast expenditure, income and cash balance over a period of time.

Doctor Proctor Bright Ideas Plc

Cash Flow Forecast

	Month 1 £	Month 2 £	Month 3 £	Month 4 £	Month 5 £	Month 6 £
Receipts						
Share issue	5,000					
Loan	3,000					
Sales receipts		4,000	5,000	6,000	7,000	7,000
Total receipts	8,000	4,000	5,000	6,000	7,000	7,000
Payments						
Salaries and wages	2,000	2,000	2,000	2,500	2,500	3,000
Rent and rates	1,000			1,000		
Power				500		
Purchase of materials	2,000	1,000	1,250	1,500	1,750	2,000
Equipment	3,500	500				2,000
Dividends						
Total payments	8,500	3,500	3,250	5,500	4,250	7,000
Receipts minus payments	(500)	500	1,750	500	2,750	0
Balance brought forward	0	(500)	0	1,750	2,250	5,000
Balance carried forward	(500)	0	1,750	2,250	5,000	5,000

4.4 THE CASH FLOW FORECAST

The cash flow forecast is used to:

1 identify sources and applications of cash
2 forecast the timing and value of the relevant cash flows.

As a planning tool the cash flow forecast identifies when extra finance may be required and when excess funds may be available for investment.

Positive and negative cash balances

Positive carried-forward balances indicate money in the bank. If the amounts are significant the money should be invested.

Negative balances indicate that current sources of finance are insufficient to cover forecast commitments. This means that arrangements will have to be made to cover the deficit.

Temporary deficits

If the deficit is temporary, it could be covered by an overdraft facility. If it seems likely to continue, management will need to extend the cash flow forecast to cover the full period for which additional finance is required.

Doctor Proctor outlines... NEW BUSINESS CASH FLOW FORECASTS

New business ventures often construct a cash flow statement for the first three years of operations.

The first year is analysed on a monthly basis, with the second and third years divided into quarters as shown below.

	Year 1												Year 2				Year 3			
	Jan	Feb	Mar	Apr	May	Jun	Jul	Aug	Se	Oct	Nov	Dec	1st	2nd	3rd	4th	1st	2nd	3rd	4th
Receipts																				
Payments																				
Balance b/fwd																				
Balance c/fwd																				

4.4 THE CASH FLOW FORECAST

The Timing of Cash Flows

Remember that if customers are allowed up to 30 days' credit before paying for supplies, then the sales for Month 1 will not be received until Month 2. Likewise it may be possible to delay the payments of suppliers.

When preparing a cash flow statement it is important to identify the point when cash is actually received or paid.

Example

Jo Newham is in the process of preparing a three-month cash flow forecast to the end of June.

The figures for her business in respect of sales and purchases are shown below.

	February	March	April	May
Sales	£10,000	£11,000	£12,000	£13,000
Purchases		£6,500	£7,000	£7,500

Jo takes 30 days' credit from her suppliers. Experience shows that 60% of her customers take 30 days to pay. The remainder pay within 60 days.

At the end of March Jo's cash balance was £5,000. She requires a cash forecast from April to June.

Phasing sales and purchases

In order to draw up her cash forecast, Jo needs to phase sales and purchases to correspond with the periods when actual cash flows will arise.

The phased cash flow chart below shows the actual timing of cash flows in and out of Jo's business.

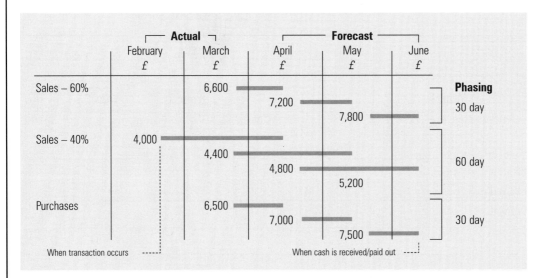

Continued

4.4 THE CASH FLOW FORECAST

Example (cont'd)

	April	May	June
	£	£	£
Sales: 60%	6,600	7,200	7,800
Sales: 40%	4,000	4,400	4,800
Purchases	− 6,500	− 7,000	− 7,500
Net cash flow	4,100	4,600	5,100
Cash b/f	5,000	9,100	13,700
Cash c/f	9,100	13,700	18,800

This is what Jo's cash flow forecast would look like up to June.

You can see that Jo is gaining a larger and larger cash balance. As I suggested earlier, she might consider how best to invest these sums!

QUESTIONS

Limiting factors

A&P Garden Products Ltd manufacture paving slabs and decorative products for the garden. Sales are seasonal and during spring and summer demand is in excess of production capacity, while in winter sales are relatively few. There is a core workforce that is supplemented with temporary labour during busy periods. The real bottleneck during the peak period is plant capacity, which cannot exceed 200 tonnes per week. The following sales forecast has been prepared by the sales manager:

	Tonnes		Tonnes
Jan	50	Feb	75
Mar	100	Apr	150
May	250	Jun	300
Jul	250	Aug	200
Sept	150		

The stock at the end of December amounted to 50 tonnes, which is the minimum stock anticipated at any point in time.

- Prepare a production budget in tonnes for the period January to September.

Variance analysis

Table A below shows an extract from the Production Expenses Budget of Red Square Ltd.

Table B shows The actual expenditure for May and the year to date.

1 Complete the report in respect of month and year-to-date budget figures.
2 Calculate the variances for each line, identifying adverse variances as a negative value.
3 Identify the variances that should be the subject of further investigation.
4 For large variances, what questions need answering?

Continued on page 67

Table A

£000s

	Jan	Feb	Mar	Apr	May	Jun
Direct wages	12.0	12.0	15.0	12.0	12.0	15.0
Salaries	6.0	6.0	6.0	6.0	6.0	6.0
Training	0.5	0.5	0.5	0.5	0.5	0.5
Welfare	0.3	0.3	0.3	0.3	0.3	0.3
Repairs and maintenance	2.5	2.5	2.5	2.5	2.5	2.5
Consumables	1.5	1.5	1.5	1.5	1.5	1.5
Depreciation	14.5	14.5	14.5	14.5	14.5	14.5
Total	37.3	37.3	40.3	37.3	37.3	40.3

Table B

£000s

May Report	Month			Year to Date		
	Actual	Budget	Variance	Actual	Budget	Variance
Direct wages	11.5			62.1		
Salaries	5.9			29.9		
Training	0.8			1.8		
Welfare	0.2			1.2		
Repairs and maintenance	5.5			17.1		
Consumables	1.8			7.4		
Depreciation	14.3			72.1		
Total	40.0			191.6		

QUESTIONS

Continued

The Cash Flow Forecast

Jit Baktar is about to set up in business as a supplier of computer equipment and network maintenance services to small firms who do not have dedicated IT staff.

He anticipates the following transactions during his first 6 months of trading:

- On 2 May he will pay into the business bank account £5,000 of his own money and £8,000 to be received as a loan from his father.
- Each month he will pay £300 for a serviced office with a small storeroom for his stocks of computer equipment.
- Starting in May, Jit is planning to gain one new service contract each month, at a value of £200 per month.
- Equipment sales should amount to £2,000 in May and are forecast to grow by £1,000 a month thereafter.

- Customers will be allowed 30 days' credit.
- Purchases of computer equipment will be £5,000 in May and thereafter at 70% of Jit's equipment sales revenue.
- Jit has been unable to arrange initial credit terms with his suppliers of computer equipment but, assuming his business is thriving, he will be given a 30-day credit period from August.
- From September, Jit plans to take on an assistant on an annual salary of £15,000.
- Other expenses for such things as telephone, motor vehicles, etc., should be around £100 per month.
- Jit intends to take drawings (his wages) during the first four months at £1,000 per month. After this period he will require £2,000 a month from the business.

1 Prepare a cash flow forecast for Jit to cover his first six months of trading.
2 Comment on the financial position of the business.

Topics covered in this unit

5.1 Introduction to Ratio Analysis
How to calculate an accounting ratio and extract ratios from the profit and loss account and balance sheet.

5.2 Return on Capital Ratios
How to calculate returns on capital employed in a business.

5.3 Profitability Ratios
How to calculate and then analyse profit margins.

5.4 Efficiency Ratios
How to compare sales with the financial resources of a business.

5.5 Shareholder Ratios
Methods of calculating returns on shares.

5.6 Gearing Ratios
How to examine company accounts in terms of the relationship between owners' capital and the capital provided by long-term loans and preference shares.

5.7 Liquidity Ratios
How to check whether a business has sufficient (or even too many) liquid assets.

5.8 Ratio Analysis in Practice
Exploring the relationship between the ratios examined in this unit.

Questions

This unit shows you how to use and apply various ratios which will help you to analyse the performance of a company. The material here is based largely on the profit and loss account on page 70 and the balance sheet on page 71.

5.1 INTRODUCTION TO RATIO ANALYSIS

For illustrative purposes, Section 5 of this book is based on data from the following financial statements of Doctor Proctor Bright Ideas Plc.

The values stated in the financial statements of a business have more meaning if they are analysed in relative terms.

As you can see, in the statements below we compare Year 2 with Year 1.

Doctor Proctor Bright Ideas Plc

Profit and Loss Account for Year 2

	Year 2	Year 1
	£000s	£000s
Turnover	1,600	1,300
Cost of sales	850	700
Gross profit	750	600
Distribution costs	150	135
Administration expenses	275	225
Operating profit	325	240
Interest paid	50	60
Profit before taxation	275	180
Corporation tax	90	60
Profit after taxation	185	120
Dividends	50	40
Retained profit for the year	135	80

Doctor Proctor Bright Ideas Plc

Balance sheet

	Year 2 £000s	Year 1 £000s
Fixed assets	1,600	1,500
Current assets:		
Stocks	425	450
Debtors	375	275
Cash		300
	800	1,025
Creditors due within one year	675	680
Net current assets	125	345
Total assets *less* current liabilities	1,725	1,845
Creditors due after one year	795	1,050
Net assets	930	795
Share capital and reserves		
Share capital (nominal value 50p)	200	200
Share premium account	350	350
Profit and loss account	380	245
	930	795

Notes to the accounts

Creditors due within one year:		
Bank overdraft	50	0
Finance lease	350	450
Trade creditors	150	130
Other creditors including taxation	125	100
Total	675	680

Creditors due after one year:		
Loan stock – Year 5	600	600
Finance lease	195	450
Total	795	1,050

5.1 INTRODUCTION TO RATIO ANALYSIS

An **accounting ratio** is a comparison of two items from the financial statement of a business:

$$\text{Ratio} = \frac{\text{Value 1}}{\text{Value 2}}$$

Many financial ratios are taken from the profit and loss account and/or the balance sheet. But remember, when using figures from the profit and loss account and balance sheet together, the profit and loss value should be an annual amount.

Method	Example
Using values from the balance sheet Ratios based on two values taken from the balance sheet can tell us a great deal about the capital structure of the business and how financial resources have been used.	Comparing **bank overdrafts** to **total finance** shows to what extent the business is relying on finance that is repayable on demand.
Using ratios from the profit and loss account Ratios based on values taken from the profit and loss account can provide useful information about profitability and reasons for changes in it.	Comparing **administration expenses** to **sales** for two successive years shows to what extent this item has contributed to an overall change in profitability.
Using ratios from the balance sheet and the profit and loss account Ratios that are based on one value from the profit and loss account and one from the balance sheet can also give us useful information about the business's financial efficiency.	Comparing the value of **debtors** to the value of **sales** shows what period of sales remain unpaid. It therefore tells us how well customer credit is being managed.

Doctor Proctor outlines... RATIOS AND BENCHMARKS

On its own, an accounting ratio has little meaning. For example, if administration costs represent 11% of sales, is this good or bad?

True analysis is only possible if a **ratio** is compared to a **benchmark**.

A benchmark may be:

– the same ratio calculated for a different period, such as the previous year. This will provide information about trends

– the same ratio calculated for comparable businesses. This will provide a means of comparing the financial performance of different companies.

Ratios may be calculated for business units within the same company, such as individual shops within a retail chain, or for similar firms trading during the same period.

A benchmark makes it possible to identify what is achievable by the most successful business or by similar businesses in the same industry.

5.2 RETURN ON CAPITAL RATIOS

Key Ideas 🔑

Calculating Financial Return

Ratios that compare profit with capital invested are an extremely useful way of measuring financial return. They allow investors to compare different companies' performance and choose the most profitable investment opportunity.

Return on equity

Just as private individuals expect a reasonable return on their savings, shareholders expect a minimum return on their investment.

The expected return will vary between companies, depending on the nature of the business and the risk associated with it.

To discover whether a company covers its cost of capital, it is necessary to calculate the **return on equity**:

Activity

The following figures are available for Bright Ideas Plc for Year 2 (*see accounts on pages 70–71*):

Return on Equity =

$$\frac{£185,000}{£930,000} \times 100\% = 19.9\%$$

Calculate the return on equity for Year 1.

Assuming shareholders expect a return of 17.5%, what do the ratios show?

Dr Proctor says:
'You Must Know This!'

Cost of capital is the financial return that investors expect.

Company directors are responsible to their shareholders – so achieving a satisfactory return on equity is a key measure of their performance and effectiveness.

Doctor Proctor Calculates

Return on Equity =

$$\frac{\text{Profit (stated after tax and preference share dividends)}}{\text{Ordinary Share Capital and Reserves}}$$

5.2 RETURN ON CAPITAL RATIOS

Key Ideas 🔑

Return On Capital Employed (ROCE)

The accounting ratio which shows how successful a company has been in covering the costs of all types of capital is termed Return On Capital Employed (ROCE).

Doctor Proctor Calculates

$$\text{ROCE} = \frac{\text{Operating Profit}}{\text{Total Capital Employed}} \times 100\%$$

From the operational management perspective, ROCE is the most significant indicator of financial performance. This is because companies generally raise finance from a number of different sources, so it is necessary for total profits to cover the total cost of capital, including debt finance.

Doctor Proctor outlines... OPERATING PROFIT AND CAPITAL EMPLOYED

Operating profit is calculated *after* deducting expenses, but *before* deducting interest payments.

Total capital employed can be calculated in two ways, both of which produce the same result:

1 The 'net asset' approach:

Fixed Assets + Stock + Debtors – Creditors (non-financing)

2 The 'sources of finance' approach:

Share Capital and Reserves + Finance Creditors (including loans, overdrafts, HP and leases) – Cash

Activity

Using the 'net asset' approach, Bright Ideas Plc's capital employed for Year 2 is calculated as follows:

	£000s
Fixed Assets	1,600
Stocks	425
Debtors	375
Less Trade Creditors	150
Other Creditors	125
	2,125

Using the 'sources of finance' approach, Bright Ideas Plc's capital employed for Year 2 is calculated as follows:

	£000s
Share Capital	930
Bank Overdraft	50
Finance Lease	545
Loan Stock	600
	2,125

$$\text{ROCE} = \frac{£325,000}{£2,125,000} \times 100\% = 15.3\%$$

Using figures from page 71, calculate the 'return on capital employed' for Year 1.

What can be deduced from these ratios?

5.3 PROFITABILITY RATIOS

Key Ideas

Measuring profitability

Profitability ratios generally take values in the profit and loss account and express them as a percentage of sales revenues.

Profit is an indication of the business's competitive position, both in respect of customers and suppliers. The ideal position is for profits to be high in relation to sales, and for competitive pressures to be weak.

Doctor Proctor Calculates

$$\text{Profit Margin} = \frac{\text{Operating Profit}}{\text{Sales}} \times 100\%$$

To assess the strength of your profitability ratios you need to compare them with those of similar firms, or with your own firm in previous time periods.

Example

The following figures are available for Bright Ideas Plc, Year 2:

$$\text{Profit margin} = \frac{325,000}{1,600,000} \times 100\% = 20.3\%$$

This would be considered a high profit margin, as many firms achieve margins of less than 10%. To judge whether this is a good performance for Bright Ideas Plc it would be necessary to take into account industry norms and the company's past performance.

DAILY NEWS

2 March 2000

Rolls Royce Delivers Consistent Growth

	1999 £m	1998 £m
Turnover	4,744	4,496
Operating profit	376	316
Profit margin	7.9%	7.0%

DAILY NEWS

2 November 2000

M&S ON THE WAY DOWN

Half Year Results

	1999 £m	1998 £m
Turnover	3,690	3,809
Operating profit	162	253
Profit margin	4.4%	6.6%

5.3 PROFITABILITY RATIOS

Key Ideas 🔑

Profit Margin Analysis

If we have greater information concerning costs, further analysis of the profit margin can be achieved by considering the items that have been deducted from turnover to arrive at operating profit.

Wages to Sales =

$$\frac{\text{Wages}}{\text{Sales}} \times 100\%$$

Activity

For Bright Ideas Plc, Year 2, the following figures are available (*see profit and loss account, page 70*):

Ratio of **Cost of Sales to Sales** =

$$\frac{£850,000}{£1,600,000} \times 100\% = 53.1\%$$

Ratio of **Distribution Cost to Sales** =

$$\frac{£150,000}{£1,600,000} \times 100\% = 9.4\%$$

Ratio of **Administration Costs to Sales** =

$$\frac{£275,000}{£1,600,000} \times 100\% = 17.2\%$$

By analysing the business's cost structure and comparing it with other businesses, it is possible to determine the efficiency of various parts of the firm.

For Bright Ideas Plc, calculate the following ratios for Year 1 (*see profit and loss account, page 70*):

a Cost of Sales to Sales

b Distribution Costs to Sales

c Administration Costs to Sales

Now compare the ratios with those for Year 2.

What conclusions can you draw?

5.4 EFFICIENCY RATIOS

Key Ideas 🔑

What is an efficiency ratio?

Whilst profitability ratios are concerned with the amount of profit relative to the value of sales, efficiency ratios are concerned with the amount of sales relative to the financial resources invested in the business.

The more capital that is tied up in a business, the greater the level of sales that need to be generated.

A large car showroom that sells hardly any cars is unlikely to be generating much profit for its owners!

Efficiency ratios measure the volume of business activity relative to the amount invested in the relevant assets of the business.

The basic formula for an efficiency ratio is:

$$\frac{\text{Volume or Value of Transactions}}{\text{Value of Assets}}$$

Dr Proctor says:
'You Must Know This!'

An efficient firm like ASDA or Tesco will want to make lots of sales (and they do). These supermarkets use a lot of capital which needs to be used efficiently.

Doctor Proctor Calculates

Like other ratios, efficiency ratios can be benchmarked against past performance and against the performance of other businesses in the same industry.

If efficiency remains constant, then any increase in investment should result in a proportionate increase in output.

In theory, efficiency ratios should be as high as possible – although in many cases there is a trade-off between volume and prices, which may affect profitability.

Learn the formulas for the following efficiency ratios:

Utilisation of Capital Employed $= \dfrac{\text{Sales}}{\text{Capital Employed}}$

Utilisation of Fixed Assets $= \dfrac{\text{Sales}}{\text{Fixed Assets}}$

Utilisation of Current Assets $= \dfrac{\text{Sales}}{\text{Current Assets}}$

5.4 EFFICIENCY RATIOS

Key Ideas 🔑

Applying efficiency ratios

Efficiency ratios can also be calculated for individual current assets and creditors within one year, but using slightly different formulas.

The basic principle of comparing trading activity with a financial resource still holds.

Formulas for calculating these separate ratios are given below.

Activity

Ratios for fixed assets can be analysed further by making separate calculations for each type of fixed asset, e.g. buildings, machinery, motor vehicles, etc.

The following figures have been extracted from the accounts of Bright Ideas Plc *(pages 70–1)*.

Year 2

Sales (turnover)	1,600
Capital employed	930
Fixed assets	1,600
Current assets	800

The ratios for Year 2 are:

$$\text{Utilisation of Capital Employed} = \frac{1,600}{930} = 1.72$$

$$\text{Utilisation of Fixed Assets} = \frac{1,600}{1,600} = 1.00$$

$$\text{Utilisation of Current Assets} = \frac{1,600}{800} = 2.00$$

Now extract the Year 1 figures for sales, capital employed, fixed assets and current assets and calculate the relevant efficiency ratios.

What do the ratios show?

Doctor Proctor Calculates

$$\text{Stock Turnover} = \frac{\text{Cost of Sales}}{\text{Stock}}$$

$$\text{Debtor Days} = \frac{\text{Debtors}}{\text{Credit Sales}} \times 365 \text{ days}$$

$$\text{Trade creditors} = \frac{\text{Creditor Days}}{\text{Cost of Sales}} \times 365 \text{ days}$$

Stock turnover is an important measure of the liquidity of a business's stocks.

Naturally it will vary between industries.

For example, a greengrocer would need to have a much higher stock turnover than a jeweller.

5.4 EFFICIENCY RATIOS

Example

	£000s
Sales (Turnover)	1,600
Cost of sales	850
Stock	425
Debtors	375
Trade creditors	150

Here are some examples to show you how efficiency ratios work out in practice.

The figures are for Bright Ideas Plc in Year 2.

Stock turnover is therefore:

$$\frac{850}{425} = 2$$

The ratio shows that stock is replenished on average twice a year. High stock turnover indicates good stock control.

Debtor days =

$$\frac{375 \times 365}{1600} = 85.5 \text{ days}$$

The ratio shows customers take on average 85.5 days to pay for supplies. Low debtor days indicates good credit control.

Creditor days =

$$\frac{150 \times 365}{850} = 64.4 \text{ days}$$

The ratio shows that Bright Ideas Plc takes on average 65.4 days to pay its suppliers.

Whilst a high ratio is good for cash flow (it is better to have cash in your own bank account rather than someone else's), it can also be an indication of cash flow problems and poor relations with suppliers.

5.5 SHAREHOLDER RATIOS

Key Ideas

Calculating the return on shares

Investors need information about the returns on different types of shares. For example, they may want to compare the returns on ordinary shares, preference shares or loan stock.

Doctor Proctor Calculates

Total Ordinary Shareholders' Return =

$$\frac{(\text{Dividend} + \text{Change in Share Price})}{\text{Share Price}} \times 100\%$$

The returns for preference shareholders and loan stockholders tend to be explicit. For example, a loan stock contract might be phrased like this:

' ... *Loan stock 8%, August 2005 will pay the holder £8 per annum for every £100 of stock owned until redemption in 2005 ...* '

The situation for ordinary shareholders is less clear. The return they receive depends on the profitability of the business, and this may be volatile over time.

Here's an easy way to calculate return on ordinary shares. Of course, it's easy to measure the return on shares after the event, but investors want to know the likelihood of a good return *before* they make their investment!

Doctor Proctor outlines... THE EARNINGS PER SHARE METHOD

One way to evaluate a company's shares is to consider the amount of profit generated for every share in issue – the so-called earnings per share approach. This is calculated as follows:

Doctor Proctor Calculates

Earnings per Share (EPS) =

$$\frac{\text{Net Profit}}{\text{Average No. of Ordinary Shares in Issue}}$$
(after Tax and Preference Dividend)

Example

For Bright Ideas Plc, profit for Year 2 is £185,000 and the number of shares is £200,000/£0.50 = 400,000.

EPS is therefore £185,000/400,000 = 46.25 pence.

This is a valuable measure, because individual shareholders clearly want to know how much profit their shares have earned. But if the company issues more shares, its profits will have to be shared out over a wider capital base. Shareholders therefore want to know that the EPS will be maintained and, if possible, increased. This can only be achieved if the company makes more profit.

5.5 SHAREHOLDER RATIOS

> **Key Ideas**
>
> **The price–earnings ratio**

A particularly useful way to measure share performance is to compare earnings per share with the share price.

Doctor Proctor Calculates

Price–Earnings Ratio =

$$\frac{\text{Share price}}{\text{Earnings per Share}}$$

If Bright Ideas Plc's share price is £4.52 at the end of Year 2:

PE Ratio =

$$\frac{£4.52}{£0.4625} = 9.8$$

The **price–earnings ratio** shows how many years it will take for current earnings to pay for a share in the company.

The variations in price–earnings ratios reflect investors' different views about the growth potential of the companies concerned.

If the outlook for growth is good, a company will command a high PE ratio (anything from 20 upwards).

A ratio under 10 indicates doubts over growth – at least in the short term.

Doctor Proctor outlines... THE DIVIDEND YIELD APPROACH

A second approach to measuring ordinary shareholders' returns is to look at the actual cash dividend paid each year. Dividends are different from profits earned because many firms retain some funds to finance future growth or to replace debt.

For Bright Ideas Plc for Year 2, the dividend per share is:

$$\frac{£50,000}{400,000 \text{ shares}} = £0.125$$

Dividend yield is therefore:

$$\frac{£0.125 \times 100\%}{£4.52} = 2.8\%$$

Clearly this is not as high as most savings accounts, but it does offer the possibility of share price appreciation.

Doctor Proctor Calculates

Dividend Yield =

$$\frac{\text{Dividend per Share}}{\text{Share Price}} \times 100\%$$

Activity

In Year 1, the ordinary share price for Bright Ideas Plc was £3.60. Calculate:

• EPS
• PE ratio
• Dividend yield.

Compare the figures with those for Year 2 *(pages 70–1)*. What conclusions can you draw?

5.6 GEARING RATIOS

Gearing ratios are concerned with the relation between:

- **capital provided by ordinary shareholders in a business**

- **capital provided in the form of loans and preference shares.**

The gearing formula

The formula on the right shows how the gearing ratio is calulated.

- **Net Debt** includes loan stock, hire purchase and finance lease agreements, loans and bank overdrafts, net of cash balances.

- **Ordinary Share Capital** includes share capital, share premium account, retained earnings and other reserves.

Gearing describes the relationship between finance that enjoys a fixed rate of return, irrespective of the fortunes of the business, and equity that enjoys profit-related returns.

The **gearing ratio** indicates the proportion of capital contributed by the real owners of the company – the ordinary shareholders. If shareholders have contributed too little capital, there is a danger that the company may have to pay crippling interest payments.

Doctor Proctor Calculates

Gearing Ratio =

$$\frac{\text{Net Debt} + \text{Preference Shares}}{\text{Ordinary Share Capital}}$$

Doctor Proctor outlines... GEARING AND INVESTMENT RISK

The way the capital of a company is structured affects the variability of the return for investors – and the degree of risk involved.

In general, investors receive financial returns in line with the risks they take. For example, in return for being first in the queue for interest and capital repayment, loan stockholders have to accept a relatively modest fixed return on their investment. Ordinary shareholders receive all the profits that are left over, because they are last in the queue.

The more finance that is raised in the form of loan stock and preference shares, the more people will

be at the head of the queue, claiming priority payment. The result will be for ordinary shareholder earnings to become more volatile.

As total profits change, the effect on the residual after paying a fixed amount of interest will be proportionartely greater – the **gearing effect**.

For shareholders, gearing will be beneficial if return on capital employed is higher than interest on loans – but it can be catastrophic if the business hits lean times.

5.6 GEARING RATIOS

Key Ideas 🔑

Calculating the gearing ratio

Let me show you how gearing can make ordinary shareholder returns more volatile.

Example

Three companies employ £100,000 of capital each.

In any one year they can generate profits in the range of £5,000–£20,000 before deducting interest on debt. Each company is financed by a different mixture of ordinary shares and debentures *(right)*.

The table below shows how differing gearing levels affect profit levels:

	Finance	
	Shares	*Debentures*
Company A	£10,000	£90,000
Company B	£50,000	£50,000
Company C	£90,000	£10,000

Company A gearing ratio is £90,000/£10,000 = **9**
Company B gearing ratio is £50,000/£50,000 = **1**
Company C gearing ratio is £10,000/£90,000 = **0.11**

Company	A	B	C
Capital structure			
Ordinary shares	10,000	50,000	90,000
Debentures at 10% p.a.	90,000	50,000	10,000
	100,000	100,000	100,000
Allocation of profits of £5,000			
Shares	–4,000	0	4,000
Debentures 10%	9,000	5,000	1,000
	5,000	5,000	5,000
Allocation of profits of £10,000			
Shares	1,000	5,000	9,000
Debentures 10%	9,000	5,000	1,000
	10,000	10,000	10,000
Allocation of profits of £20,000			
Shares	11,000	15,000	19,000
Debentures 10%	9,000	5,000	1,000
	20,000	20,000	20,000

Continued

5.6 GEARING RATIOS

Example (cont'd)

Whatever the level of profits, debenture-holders will always receive 10% of the value of debentures, e.g. £9,000 when £90,000 of debentures have been issued. However, the percentage returns enjoyed by ordinary shareholders varies widely, being dependent on gearing in addition to the level of profits.

Taking the nine scenarios from above, the percentage returns to ordinary shareholders are:

Company	A	B	C	
Gearing	9	1	0.11	i.e. volatile, risky: possible high profits or heavy losses
On profits of £5,000	– 40%	0%	4.4%	
On profits of £10,000	10%	10%	10%	
On profits of £20,000	110%	30%	21.1%	
Range of returns	150%	30%	16.7%	more certainty of a modest return

In general, ratios under 0.25 indicate low gearing and values in excess of 1 show high gearing.

Interest cover

Another valuable measure of financial risk is the relationship of interest payments to the profits generated by the business.

This is known as **interest cover**. The larger the interest cover, the less risk in the future of interest payments pushing the business into a loss.

Doctor Proctor Calculates

$$\textbf{Interest Cover} = \frac{\text{Profit before Interest}}{\text{Interest Paid}}$$

Activity

Using the figures above for Companies A, B and C, the following interest cover ratios can be calculated when profit before interest is £10,000:

		Interest cover
Company A	$\dfrac{£10,000}{£9,000}$	= **1.11**
Company B	$\dfrac{£10,000}{£5,000}$	= **2**
Company C	$\dfrac{£10,000}{£1,000}$	= **10**

Calculate the gearing ratio and interest cover for Bright Ideas Plc for Years 1 and 2 *(see pages 70–1)*.

Evaluate the figures. What conclusions can you draw?

5.7 LIQUIDITY RATIOS

Key Ideas 🔑

Defining liquidity

Liquidity = The ease with which an asset can be turned into cash.

> **Dr Proctor says:**
> **'You Must Know This!'**
>
> Remember that however profitable a business may be, it must always have enough working capital to provide the liquidity to pay its suppliers and employees on a day-to-day basis.

Doctor Proctor outlines... CURRENT RATIO AND ACID TEST RATIO

Two ratios that are commonly used to measure financial liquidity are the **current ratio** and the more stringent **acid test ratio**.

Whereas the current ratio simply compares current assets to short-term creditors, the acid-test ratio compares *only* cash and other monetary assets to short-term creditors.

Monetary assets are those with an obvious cash value (e.g. trade debtors who will payin the next month or so) and investments in the form of securities that can be readily traded and converted to cash.

Doctor Proctor Calculates

Current ratio =

$$\frac{\text{Current Assets}}{\text{Creditors Due In Less Than One Year}}$$

Doctor Proctor Calculates

Acid-test ratio =

$$\frac{\text{Current Assets} - \text{Stock}}{\text{Creditors Due In Less Than One Year}}$$

Activity

The following figures are available for Bright Ideas Plc for Year 2:

Current ratio = $\dfrac{800}{675}$ = 1.18

Acid-test ratio = $\dfrac{375}{675}$ = 0.6

Using the figures given above for Bright Ideas Plc, calculate the ratios for Year 1 (*see page 71*).

5.7 LIQUIDITY RATIOS

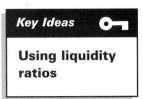

Key Ideas

Using liquidity ratios

The higher a business's liquidity ratio, the more assets are available to pay the firm's creditors.

But high ratios may indicate that excessive funds are being tied up in working capital, thus reducing return on capital employed.

Monitoring change

A change in the ratios may be due to a change in assets or a change in liabilities. It is important to know the exact cause, because this will determine whether the change is for the better or for the worse.

For example, a reduction in the current ratio could be caused by either a reduction in stocks due to improved stock control or an increase in liabilities.

What is an ideal liquidity ratio?

A current ratio of 2.0 and an acid-test ratio of 1.0 are much-quoted benchmarks, but it is difficult to generalise about an 'ideal' value for either ratio.

For businesses with strong, consistent cash flows, such as food retailers, there is less need for funds to be held as working capital and ratios are often significantly below those for – say – engineering firms.

Unilever 1999

Current ratio 1:5

Acid test ratio 1:1

Sainsbury's 1999

Current ratio 0.73

Acid test ratio 0.66

Current and acid test ratios for two financially strong companies

5.8 RATIO ANALYSIS IN PRACTICE

Key Ideas 🔑

Accounts for shareholders

Accounting ratios should be seen as forming a hierarchy. More can be discovered about a particular ratio by 'drilling down' to a level of greater detail.

As you can see:

- a change in **ROCE** is caused by a change in profit margin and/ or utilisation of capital employed
- a change in **profit margin** is caused by a change in gross profit margin and/or expenses to sales
- a change in **total expenses to sales** is caused by a change in the individual expense types to sales.

The diagram here shows how the hierarchy of accounting ratios is arranged.

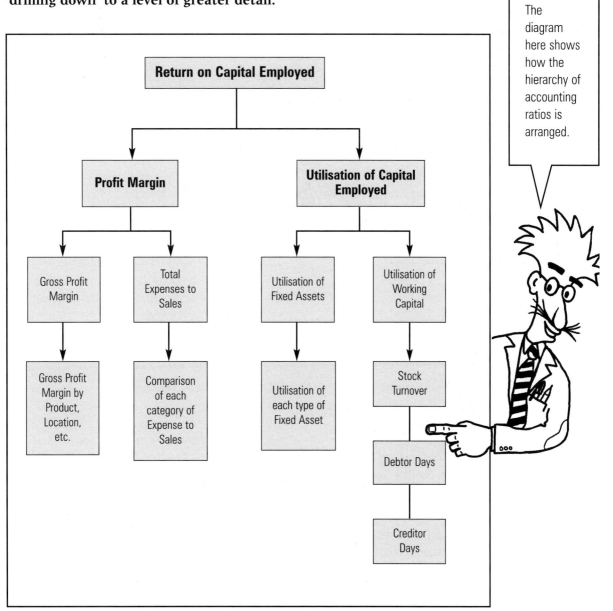

5.8 RATIO ANALYSIS IN PRACTICE

Key Ideas

Limitations of ratio analysis

2
The external financial analyst has to use information that is at least several months old.

Ratio analysis is a powerful tool but it has its drawbacks: Here are some of them …

3
In order for ratio analysis to be carried out in full, published accounts must provide enough detail to work on.

1
Financial performance indicators place emphasis on short-term results. Ratios such as 'earnings per share' and 'return on capital employed' are subject to accounting conventions that might deter businesses from pursuing policies that are in their long-term interests.

For example, most expenditure on research and development, and all staff welfare costs (including training) are charged against the current year's profits, even though the benefits may not be realised for some years to come.

4
Comparison of ratios between companies is difficult, as the business activities of different firms are rarely identical.

5
Some values may be affected more than others by changes in price levels. In particular, the value of property used in the business will depend very much on when it was purchased. Low property valuations will result in artificially high returns on capital employed.

Doctor Proctor outlines... LIKE-FOR-LIKE COMPARISONS

Valuations in the balance sheet depend on the accounting policies adopted. Where different businesses are compared, the accounts of each should be restated on a **like-for-like basis** before ratios are calculated.

For example, the depreciation rates for fixed assets and the basis for the valuation of stocks need to be checked for consistency, because companies can and often do present information differently.

Despite the difficulties, however, and the care that must be taken in their use, ratios provide a coherent structure by which to analyse accounts. Correctly used, they provoke searching questions that should result in tighter control and a better understanding of the business.

QUESTIONS

The accounts shown below and on page 90 relate to Red Ltd and Blue Ltd, two companies operating in different industry segments.
One company is a clothes retailer, the other an engineering firm.

1 Calculate the following ratios for each business for each year:

   i)   Gross profit margin
   ii)   Operating profit margin
   iii) Return on capital employed
   iv)   Stock turnover (base usage on 'cost of sales')
   v)   Debtor days
   vi)   Current ratio
   vii) Interest cover.

2 Identify for each company whether the ratios improved or deteriorated in Year 2.

3 Both companies experienced a fall in operating profits. Give reasons for the deterioration in Year 2 financial performance. What does this tell us about likely future performance?

Continued on page 90

Red Ltd and Blue Ltd
Profit and Loss Accounts for the Year Ended 31 December 200x

| | Red Ltd | | Blue Ltd | |
| | Year 1 | Year 2 | Year 1 | Year 2 |
	£000s	£000s	£000s	£000s
Turnover	7,900	8,000	4,900	5,500
Cost of sales	4,050	4,300	2,650	3,050
Gross profit	3,850	3,700	2,250	2,450
Distribution costs	2,000	2,150	550	450
Administration expenses	1,100	1,200	900	950
Exceptional item	–	–	–	350
Operating profit	750	350	800	700
Interest payable	200	250	250	300
Profit before tax	550	100	550	400
Taxation	200	30	125	100
Profit after tax	350	70	425	300
Dividends	200	100	75	100
Retained profit	150	– 30	350	200
Profit and loss account b/f	475	625	375	725
Profit and loss account c/f	625	595	725	925

Note:
The exceptional item for Blue Ltd was in respect of staff redundancy costs following the streamlining of distribution operations half way through Year 2.

QUESTIONS

Continued

4   Both companies experienced an increase in short-term finance creditors. What factors contributed to this situation?

5   Summarise the financial position of each business.

6   Which company is the retailer and which the engineering firm?

Red Ltd and Blue Ltd

Balance Sheets as at 31 December 200X

	Red Ltd		Blue Ltd	
	Year 1	Year 2	Year 1	Year 2
	£000s	£000s	£000s	£000s
Fixed assets	3,900	3,750	3,500	3,550
Current assets				
Stocks	600	800	550	500
Debtors	25	50	700	1,050
Cash	100	0	50	0
	725	850	1,300	1,550
Creditors due within one year				
Finance creditors	200	805	200	350
Trade creditors	500	550	450	400
Other creditors	200	150	250	250
	900	1,505	900	1,000
Net current assets/liabilities	– 175	– 655	400	550
	3,725	3,095	3,900	4,100
Creditors due after one year				
Finance creditors	1,000	500	2,000	2,000
Net assets	2,625	2,595	1,900	2,100
Capital and reserves				
Share capital	1,000	1,000	500	500
Share premium account	1,000	1,000	675	675
Profit and loss account	625	595	725	925
	2,625	2,595	1,900	2,100

UNIT 6
COSTS AND DECISION-MAKING

This unit covers the important topic of costing. It shows how different costing approaches can be used by managers to make key planning decisions – such as which goods and services to produce with existing resources.

Topics covered in this unit

6.1 Introduction to Costing
Defining management accounting, cost units and cost centres.

6.2 Direct and Indirect Costs
Examples of direct costs that can be attributed to cost units, and indirect costs which cannot be attributed in this way.

6.3 Absorption Costing
How profits made by a business can be related to specific products or activities.

6.4 Fixed and Variable Costs
How some costs can be related to the level of business activity (variable costs), while others (fixed costs) do not change with the level of business activity.

6.5 Marginal Costing
An approach to short-term decision-making based on changes in costs produced by small increases in output.

6.6 Break-Even Analysis
How to calculate the break-even point of a business and how such information can be used in decision-making.

6.7 Activity-Based Costing
How to attribute costs according to how they are incurred.

6.8 Costing Summary
The key aspects of absorption, marginal and activity-based costing; how the different methods are used.

Questions

6.1 INTRODUCTION TO COSTING

So far, we have been looking at the reporting of historical financial performance. This is very important because it helps us to see how well the managers have managed the business. As we have seen, published financial reports examining profit and cash flow tend to look at the business as a whole.

What we now need to look at is financial information concerning **individual products, processes and departments.** This is the information managers use in order to carry out day-to-day activities and plan for the future.

Management accounting provides managers with the information they need for planning. It focuses on the 'micro' aspects of the business, looking at the incidence of cost in relation to business activity.

Doctor Proctor outlines... COST INFORMATION

The purpose of cost information is:

1 to measure the cost of providing a particular product or service
2 to measure the cost of different parts of the business
3 to allow managers to monitor performance and control activities
4 to satisfy financial reporting requirements in terms of the valuation of stocks
5 to enable managers to evaluate alternatives – for example, the cost of further investment in plant and machinery.

Analysing Costs

Costs can be broken down into three categories:

1 **Labour costs** are payments to the business's employees
2 **Materials** are the physical goods consumed in making a supply to a customer
3 **Expenses** are the costs of all the other resources consumed, e.g. rent and the services of other businesses.

Comparing historical cost against a benchmark enables management to control adverse trends. An understanding of how costs are incurred also helps future planning and decision-making.

6.1 INTRODUCTION TO COSTING

> **Key Ideas** 🔑
>
> **Matching costs to products**

Cost is measured in terms of the money used to buy a particular resource. However, linking costs to a particular part of a business, or to a particular product, is not always easy.

Business operations often have many different products and processes that share resources. The problem is how to divide common costs between cost objects.

For example, the Mars confectionery factory at Slough not only produces Mars Bars, but also Snickers, Maltesers and many other lines. It is not always easy to divide costs such as the costs of power, rent and business rates between these different products.

> Generally a cost can be identified with **one** of these two categories of **cost object**.

Cost units
A cost unit is a measure of a firm's output. For example, for Marks & Spencer, a sweater or a pair of socks would be a cost unit. For British Airways, a passenger mile would be a cost unit. If a business can quantify the total cost of one unit, this can be a basis for setting its sales price.

Cost centres
A cost centre is part of the structure of an organisation. Costs that cannot be linked to cost units are linked to the department or section of the organisation that incurs them. In a hotel, a typical cost centre would be the kitchen or laundry.

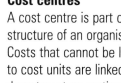

Distinguish Between ...

6.2 DIRECT AND INDIRECT COSTS

Key Ideas

Categories of cost

Direct costs are costs that can be attributed and recorded against a specific cost unit.

For example, in producing a range of chocolate bars, it is possible to identify and record the direct costs of the materials that go into each type of bar.

Dr Proctor says:
'You Must Know This!'

Some costs (direct costs) are easy to link to cost units – for example, the cost of the chocolate used to make a Mars bar. Other costs (indirect costs) cannot be linked in this way.

Indirect costs cannot be attributed to specific cost units, and so are recorded against the appropriate cost centre.

For example, in a confectionery plant it would be impossible to work out how much of the lighting was used directly for the production of one type of chocolate bar and how much for another type.

Doctor Proctor outlines... EXAMPLES OF DIRECT COSTS

The main types of direct costs are:

1 Labour
The term **direct labour** (or **direct wages**) is used to describe payments to workers who make specific products or provide specific services.

A confectionery firm such as Cadbury will pay direct wages to chocolate line operators, and an office-cleaning firm will pay direct wages to its cleaners.

2 Materials
Direct material is the cost of material used to make specific products or services.

Cadbury may require materials in the form of cocoa and sugar; the cleaning firm will need chemicals and materials for specific cleaning contracts.

3 Expenses
Direct expenses are other costs incurred specifically in the course of providing a product or service. These include royalty payments that are based on unit volumes and the cost of sub-contractors directly working on cost units.

Thus, the prime costs of producing an Easter egg with a picture of David Beckham on it would comprise the direct labour and direct materials involved in producing the eggs, plus the royalty paid to David Beckham for the use of his picture (per egg made or sold).

6.2 DIRECT AND INDIRECT COSTS

Doctor Proctor outlines... INDIRECT COSTS

Costs that are not direct costs are classified as **indirect costs**. These cannot be attributed to specific cost units, either because they are unrelated or because it is impractical to do so.

For example, an engineering firm may decide to treat consumables such as rags and lubricating oils as a cost-centre expense (i.e. an indirect cost) because the amounts concerned are insignificant.

1 Labour

Indirect labour costs are wages and salaries paid to employees *while they are not making cost units*. This includes payments to staff engaged in general management, administration and distribution, and wages of workers who do not actually perform direct work – for example, maintenance engineers – or who may have enforced idle time between direct jobs.

2 Materials

Indirect materials include items that are too low in value to be linked to specific products, e.g. lubricating materials, rags for cleaning down machines and small nuts and bolts.

3 Expenses

Indirect expenses include a wide range of costs, including property rents, power, stationery and depreciation of fixed assets. Indirect costs are often called **overheads** and are usually analysed into **production, administration and distribution** costs.

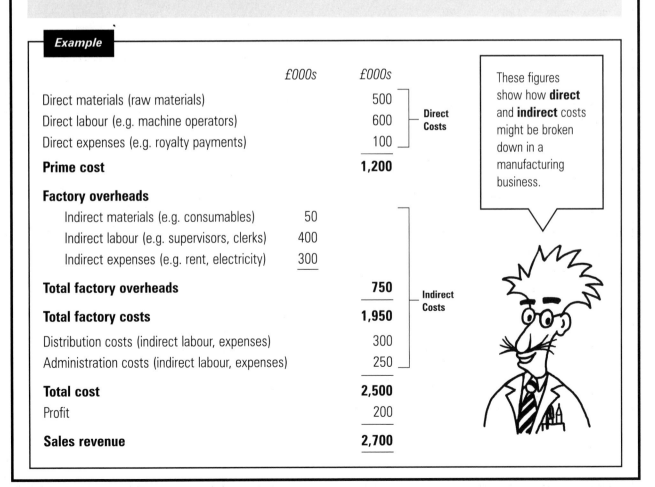

Example

	£000s	£000s	
Direct materials (raw materials)		500	
Direct labour (e.g. machine operators)		600	Direct Costs
Direct expenses (e.g. royalty payments)		100	
Prime cost		**1,200**	
Factory overheads			
Indirect materials (e.g. consumables)	50		
Indirect labour (e.g. supervisors, clerks)	400		
Indirect expenses (e.g. rent, electricity)	300		
Total factory overheads		**750**	Indirect Costs
Total factory costs		**1,950**	
Distribution costs (indirect labour, expenses)		300	
Administration costs (indirect labour, expenses)		250	
Total cost		**2,500**	
Profit		200	
Sales revenue		**2,700**	

These figures show how **direct** and **indirect** costs might be broken down in a manufacturing business.

6.3 ABSORPTION COSTING

Key Ideas 🔑

Allocating costs in a multi-product firm

The profitability of a business depends on the relationship between total business income and total business costs. This information is contained in the profit and loss account.

But management also need to understand how individual products contribute towards a firm's profitability. This is not easy for the multi-product firm, as indirect costs relate to more than one product.

Example

A market trader makes the following sales:

	Sales £	Cost £	Gross profit £
9 sweaters	180	120	60
5 scarves	25	20	5
2 coats	80	45	35
	285	185	100

The market stall costs £40 to rent for the day, so net profit for the day is just £60.

But how should the rent be allocated to the individual product ranges so that it can be seen which products contributed to the £60 profit?

The answer is to apply the principle of **absorption costing**.

In this example, the rent could be absorbed in a number of different ways:

1. between sweaters, scarves and coats equally (£13.33 each)

2. in proportion to sales revenue (180/25/80)

3. as a % mark-up on direct cost (24.3%)

4. in proportion to space devoted to each product – say, sweaters (60%), scarves (10%), and coats (30%).

How would the £60 final profit be analysed between the various products using each of the methods of absorbing rent described above?

Sweater £20.00

Scarf £5.00

Coat £40.00

6.3 ABSORPTION COSTING

Key Ideas 🔑

Stages of absorption costing

In more complex businesses there may be numerous cost centres where indirect costs are incurred. In order to allocate those costs, absorption costing has to be broken down into a number of stages.

Pool of Overheads

Stage 1
Share out costs to cost centres

| Specific to a particular department (e.g. indirect workers, travel costs)? | General business cost (e.g. insurance, rent, canteen subsidy)? |

Allocate   **Apportion**

Dept. A   **Dept. B**   **Dept. C**

Stage 2
Identify measure of departmental activity

Calculate measure of activity (e.g. labour hours)

Stage 3
Calculate overhead cost for each unit of production

Calculate cost per hour

Calculate product cost

6.3 ABSORPTION COSTING

Key Ideas

The stages of cost apportionment

Let's take a closer look at the stages of the absorption costing process.

1

Overhead costs are shared out to the various cost centres as fairly as possible. Where costs are known to have been incurred by a specific department, e.g. the wages of its indirect workers, they are allocated accordingly.

If costs cannot be allocated to individual production cost centres – e.g. rent that is paid for the whole business or support functions such as the stores that service a number of production cost centres – they are shared out as fairly as possible.

This process is called **cost apportionment**. It is usually based on an agreed measure relevant to the way the cost is incurred, such as floor area, or the number of stores requisitions for each production cost centre, etc.

2

Once all production overheads have been allocated or apportioned to the production departments, the next step is to include these costs in the total costs of the products made.

The process of including overheads in product costs is called **overhead absorption**. It is achieved by finding a measure for departmental activity – for example, labour hours or machine hours.

3

The overhead for each unit of production is costed.

For example, assuming an overhead recovery rate of £50 per machine hour, a product requiring 2 hours' machine time would incur an overhead of £100 (2 x £50).

Doctor Proctor Calculates

A **cost per hour** can be calculated by dividing overheads by the number of hours worked.

For example, production overheads of £50,000 and machine hours of 1,000 would result in an overhead recovery rate of £50 per machine hour.

6.3 ABSORPTION COSTING

Choosing a method of apportionment

In practice there are many methods of apportionment that can be used in a particular situation. Measures can include:

- number of employees
- number of stores requisitions
- units of energy consumed

You simply need to think clearly about which will be the most appropriate.

Common sense needs to be used when deciding how to apportion costs. In any business, financial managers should consider the most logical way of apportioning costs. The approach will vary according to the nature of the business and its activities.

The cost of subsidising a staff canteen could be apportioned pro rata according to staff numbers

Doctor Proctor outlines... OVERHEAD ABSORPTION CALCULATIONS

There are three widely recognised bases for **overhead absorption rate (OAR)** calculations.

The formulas for these are given below.

Doctor Proctor Calculates

1 Direct Wage OAR $= \dfrac{\text{Overheads}}{\text{Direct Wages}}$

2 Direct Labour Hours OAR $= \dfrac{\text{Overheads}}{\text{Direct Labour Hours}}$

3 Machine Hours OAR $= \dfrac{\text{Overheads}}{\text{Machine Hours}}$

When choosing an absorption base, the guiding principle is that it should be a fair measure of activity of the particular department.

For example, overheads of a printing press manned by a number of workers could be absorbed using a 'printing press hours' rate, while overheads for a manual packing process could be absorbed using a 'labour hours' rate.

6.4 FIXED AND VARIABLE COSTS

Key Ideas 🔑

How costs vary with business activity

Dr Proctor says:
'You Must Know This!'

Some costs vary with the level of business activity, while others are fixed.

The table below shows how costs can be classified according to the way in which they are incurred

Cost Type	Examples	Illustration
Fixed costs remain unchanged as business activity varies.	Property rents; interest payable on loans	Cost — Fixed costs — / Activity
Variable costs change in direct proportion to the level of business activity.	Materials used in the manufacture of products; salesperson's commissions	Cost — Variable costs / Activity
Semi-variable costs contain fixed and variable elements.	Vehicle maintenance costs (some costs such as the MOT certificate are fixed, while others vary with levels of use, such as the cost of replacing tyres)	Cost — Semi-variable costs / Activity
Stepped costs are costs that are fixed for a range of business volume, but which jump to a new level when volume increases beyond a certain point.	Supervision wages; plant and equipment (as production levels increase, plant and equipment may have to be added to or upgraded)	Cost — Stepped costs / Activity

6.4 FIXED AND VARIABLE COSTS

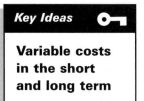

Key Ideas 🔑

Variable costs in the short and long term

Care must be taken when classifying costs between fixed and variable.

In the long run, *all* costs can be considered as variable, since there is always a possibility of the business closing down altogether.

However, in the short term, very few costs are actually variable. Most are unavoidable, particularly if there is a contractual agreement to incur them.

For example, direct workers only represent a variable cost in the short term if they are paid on a **piecework** basis.

Where there is a contractual obligation to pay wages on a time-period basis (e.g. an annual salary), wages are a **fixed cost** in the short term.

Doctor Proctor outlines... FIXED OR STEPPED COSTS?

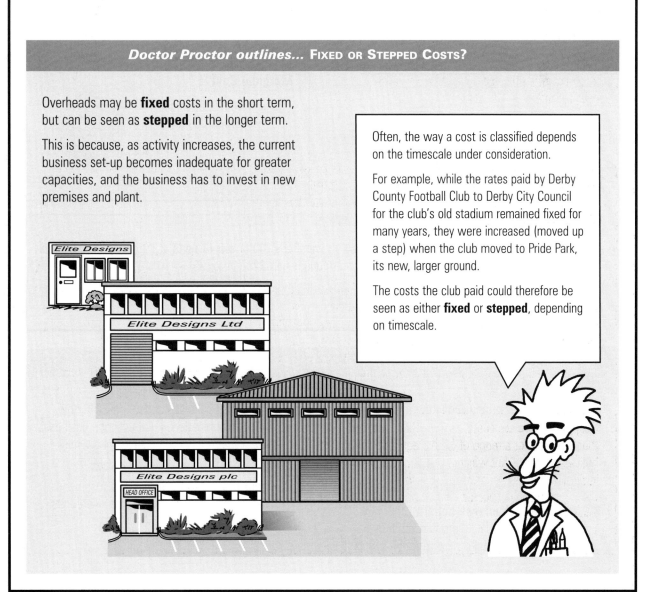

Overheads may be **fixed** costs in the short term, but can be seen as **stepped** in the longer term.

This is because, as activity increases, the current business set-up becomes inadequate for greater capacities, and the business has to invest in new premises and plant.

Often, the way a cost is classified depends on the timescale under consideration.

For example, while the rates paid by Derby County Football Club to Derby City Council for the club's old stadium remained fixed for many years, they were increased (moved up a step) when the club moved to Pride Park, its new, larger ground.

The costs the club paid could therefore be seen as either **fixed** or **stepped**, depending on timescale.

6.5 MARGINAL COSTING

Key Ideas 🔑

What is marginal costing?

Marginal costing is a tool for short-term decision-making which looks at how additional output contributes to fixed costs and profits.

> Here's my method of calculating whether an additional unit of output will increase contribution.

When we refer to the **margin**, we are talking about *additional units of output*.

For example, if a business increases output from 100 to 101 units, the **marginal unit** is the 101st unit. The **marginal cost** is thus the cost of producing the 101st unit, and the **marginal revenue** is the revenue from that 101st unit.

Doctor Proctor Calculates

Change in Contribution =

Marginal Revenue − Marginal Cost

Marginal Revenue =

Change in Total Revenue

Marginal Cost =

Variable Cost + Increase in Stepped Costs

Example

If a business can sell 10 units for £100 or sell 11 units at £95, then the marginal revenue for the eleventh unit is just £45 (11 x £95) − (10 x £100).

In this case, if the marginal cost is less than £45, selling the extra 11 units will increase contribution.

Doctor Proctor outlines... WHEN TO USE MARGINAL COSTING

Marginal costing is often used in the following situations:

1 **Make or buy?** For example, when a business needs to decide whether to manufacture a product in-house or sub-contract to a supplier.

2 **Terminate a business activity?** Part of a business or a particular product line may be reporting losses under the absorption costing system. The business needs to find out how closure or termination will affect total business profits. What costs will be saved and what revenues lost?

3 **Setting the selling price**. A business needs to know where to pitch the selling price of its products.

6.5 MARGINAL COSTING

Key Ideas 🔑

Which costs are relevant to marginal costing?

Any item of cost which is likely to change if output changes must be taken into account in marginal costing.

It is also important not to overlook **opportunity costs** –the benefits that have to be sacrificed in choosing one course of action rather than another.

If a cost has already been incurred, then it is not relevant to a marginal costing decision – it is referred to as a **sunk cost**.

Unavoidable costs, i.e. costs that will be incurred irrespective of the decision to be made, are also not relevant.

Activity

Jill runs a stall selling fruit and vegetables at the local market. Before the day begins, she purchases 100kg of bananas for £50. During the day, she sells 90kg of bananas for £90. The left-over bananas will not keep until next week's market, but a local shop will take them for 25p/kg. She has already agreed to hire a hand trolley for £2 to move any unsold stock she may have.

In the final minutes of trading, what is the minimum price Jill should charge for the remaining 10kg of bananas?

Answer

In order to reach a pricing decision, Jill must first think about what costs are relevant.

* The purchase price of the bananas is not relevant as it represents a **sunk cost**.

* The trolley hire is an **unavoidable** cost (assuming the arrangement cannot be cancelled) and so is not relevant.

* There are no additional cost to be incurred, so the only cost is the **opportunity cost** of not selling to the local grocer.

Hence the minimum price should be 25p/kg.

6.6 BREAK-EVEN ANALYSIS

Key Ideas 🔑

Calculating the break-even point

The break-even point is the point at which sales levels are high enough not to make a loss, but not high enough to make a profit.

In other words, sales revenues just cover costs. In order for a business to survive, it must know know how many units it needs to sell to break even.

Doctor Proctor Calculates

The break-even point can be calculated as follows:

Break-even Point in Sales Units =

$$\frac{\text{Fixed costs}}{\text{Contribution per Unit}}$$

where **Contribution per Unit** =

Selling Price – Variable Cost

Example

In order to raise finance for her car repair business, Kirsty Jones is preparing a business plan to present to her bank manager.

She wants to show how many customers she needs to attract each week in order to break even. Fixed costs are estimated to be £400 a week and a typical repair at £120 will incur material costs of £40.

Contribution per Customer =

£120 – £40 = £80

Break-even point $= \dfrac{£400}{£80}$

= 5 customers per week.

Sales Value at Break-even =

Number of Customers x Sales Price

= 5 x 120

= £600

All start-up businesses will want to know at what point they will **break even**, i.e. cover their costs through sales revenues.

Continued

6.6 BREAK-EVEN ANALYSIS

Constructing a break-even chart

A good way of identifying the break-even point is to use a graph or chart.

The example below is based on the figures for Kirsty Jones on page 104.

Example (cont'd)

Customer Nos.	Fixed cost £	Variable cost £	Total cost £	Sales value £
2	400	80	480	240
4	400	160	560	480
6	400	240	640	720
8	400	320	720	960

Step 1

The first stage is to quantify costs and revenues at different volumes of sales.

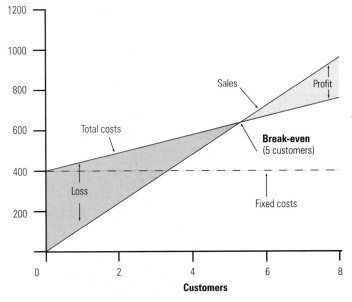

Step 2

The next step is to plot fixed costs, total cost and sales revenue against business activity – in this case, numbers of repairs.

The point at which the lines for sales revenue and total cost intersect is the break-even point.

At sales volumes to the left of the break-even point, the vertical gap between sales and total cost lines represents the loss made. To the right of the break-even point, the gap between the two lines represents profit.

6.6 BREAK-EVEN ANALYSIS

Key Ideas 🔑

The margin of safety

The break-even point is a very useful financial indicator. It can be compared with *anticipated* volumes to test the viability of a business plan, and with *actual* activity to monitor a business's performance.

The difference between planned or current volumes and the break-even point represents the **margin of safety**. This can be expressed as a percentage.

Doctor Proctor Calculates

Margin of Safety =

$$\frac{\text{Actual Volume} - \text{Break-even Volume}}{\text{Actual Volume}}$$

Taking the Kirsty Jones example (page 104), if Kirsty anticipated 7 customers a week, the margin of safety would be:

$$\frac{7-5}{5} = 40\%$$

Example

Patak's Spices currently produces 5,000 packets of mixed spice per month. Using figures for cost and revenue, it can be seen that the business will break even on 2,500 units. The margin of safety is therefore:

$$\frac{5,000 - 2,500}{5,000} = 50\%$$

The margin of safety for Patak's Spices can also be represented graphically by the horizontal difference in the diagram below.

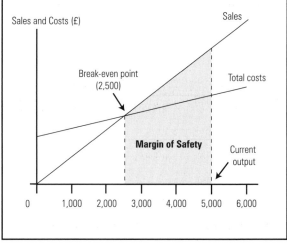

Doctor Proctor outlines... MATCHING TARGET SALES TO TARGET PROFIT

Using the formula below, it is possible to calculate the level of sales needed to attain a target profit.

Number of Sales Units Needed to Attain Target Profit =

$$\frac{\text{Fixed Costs} + \text{Profit}}{\text{Contribution per Unit}}$$

Referring back to the example on page 104, we can now calculate how many customers Kirsty Jones needs in order to make £240 profit per week:

Number of Sales Units =

$$\frac{£400 + £240}{£80}$$

= 8 customers per week

6.7 ACTIVITY-BASED COSTING

Techniques for costing indirect items (overheads) are concerned with attributing shared costs to individual product lines or customer orders. The two principal methods are **absorption costing** and **activity-based costing**.

- **Absorption costing** shares costs among a business's product lines or customer orders according to the amount of machine or direct labour time they require.

- **Activity-Based Costing (ABC)** is concerned with attributing costs according to how they are incurred.

Activity-based costing became widely used in the early 1990s, when indirect costs represented a rising proportion of total costs.

At this time new manufacturing techniques were also leading to:

- reduced labour costs
- higher capital costs and other indirect costs
- greater emphasis on a salaried workforce, with labour representing a fixed cost in the short term
- higher product specifications, with raw materials representing a lower proportion of total product costs.

Doctor Proctor outlines... ACTIVITY-BASED COSTING

Activity-based costing attempts to explain the link between products and the costs that are incurred during their production or manufacture.

The ABC process comprises five main stages:

1 Identification of the **activities** that take place in the organisation

2 Identification of the **cost driver** (i.e. the activity that incurs the cost) for each major activity

3 Establishment of a **cost centre** or **cost pool** for each major activity

4 Calculation of a **cost driver rate** for each cost pool, as follows:

$$\text{Cost Driver Rate} = \frac{\text{Cost Pool}}{\text{Volume of Cost Drivers}}$$

5 **Linking of product lines** to the **cost of activities, according to their demand for those activities** (as measured by the cost drivers).

For a practical example of how the process of activity-based costing might be carried out, see pages 108–9.

6.7 ACTIVITY-BASED COSTING

Here's how the five stages of activity-based costing might be carried out in a typical supermarket.

Example

Stage 1 *Identification of the activities that take place in the organisation*	In a supermarket, these might include: • purchasing goods • distributing and storing goods • displaying goods • processing goods (e.g. in the in-store bakery and meat counter) • processing sales.

Stage 2 *Identification of the cost driver (i.e. the activity that incurs the cost) for each major activity*	*Activity*	*Cost Drivers*
	Purchasing	**Number of purchase orders and quality inspections**. For example, quality control of fresh produce will be more time-consuming and frequent than for tinned products.
	Distribution	**Product volume, number of deliveries required, number of crates to be handled and storage conditions**. For example, the storage and distribution of dairy and meat products is more onerous than for dried goods such as pasta and rice.
	Display	**Product volume, number of individual items that require handling**. Analysis of these will show that big products require a lot of expensive shelf space and that multi-packs are cheaper to handle than single packs.
	**Sales processing** (i.e. checkouts and customer service)	**Number of customers, number of items, product weight, product volume** In general, bulky goods like toilet paper and bags of potatoes will take more time to handle through the sales checkouts than smaller items such as confectionery and cheese, despite often being less in value. ABC will demonstrate that it is less time-consuming – and hence cheaper – to sell £100 of groceries to one customer than sell £10 worth to 10 customers.

Continued

6.7 ACTIVITY-BASED COSTING

Example (cont'd)

Stage 3

Establishment of a cost centre or cost pool for each major activity

Costs are now allocated to each of the activities identified above. Wages and salaries, property, vehicles and other costs are account-coded to each of the activities identified.

Stage 4

Calculation of cost driver rates for each cost pool

For example, let us assume from **3** above that:

- each hour of check-out time costs £30
- each sales item takes 5 seconds to be scanned
- each customer takes 2 minutes to pay and finish packing.

Cost driver rate per customer = £1 (£30 x 2 minutes/60 minutes)

Cost driver rate per item = 4.2p (£30 x 5 seconds/(60 minutes x 60 seconds))

Stage 5

Linking of product lines to the cost of activities, according to their demand for those activities (as measured by the cost drivers)

To calculate the cost of a customer or product, the relevant cost driver rates are applied and added to direct costs.

For example, using the figures above, it is possible to make the following comparison:

- Sales processing costs for **1** customer who purchases **20** items = £1 + (20 x 4.2p) = **£1.84**

- Sales processing cost of a customer with just 10 items = **£1.42**

Traditional cost systems which apply a common unit cost rate tend to overstate the cost of high-volume orders and understate the cost of low-volume orders. Activity-based costing presents a much more accurate picture. In this case, for example, it might be used to justify loyalty schemes that increase the spend per customer as well as attracting more customers.

6.8 COSTING SUMMARY

Three approaches to costing

In this section we've been looking at the three techniques of absorption costing, marginal costing and activity-based costing. Here's a recap of the key points.

1
Absorption costing considers the distinction between direct and indirect costs. It is primarily concerned with how indirect costs can be shared between individual products and/or customers.

2
Marginal costing is interested in how costs change as business activity changes. It is therefore concerned with analysing costs into short-term fixed and variable.

3
Through its use of cost drivers, **activity-based costing** has some similarities with both absorption costing and marginal costing. Like absorption costing it is concerned with how indirect costs can be attributed to individual products and/or customers. Like marginal costing, it is concerned with the variability of cost.

Unlike absorption costing, however, it shares cost according to a product's demand for activity. It also considers that nearly all costs are discretionary (and hence variable) over the long term (after all, the business could be wound up).

6.8 COSTING SUMMARY

Each of the three costing methods is based on the following simple formulations:

Total Cost = Direct Costs + Indirect Costs
Total Cost = Variable Costs + Fixed Costs

But remember that the classifications 'direct/ indirect' and 'variable/fixed' are not interchangeable!

Direct/indirect and fixed/variable

Direct material costs are **variable** costs, but in the case of direct labour, the classification depends on the basis for remuneration. Only the payment of wages directly linked to the work being considered, such as those paid to sessional and piece-rate workers, are truly variable.

Many **indirect** costs are **fixed** (at least in the short term) – although they may also include some variable costs. In the case of electricity costs in a manufacturing plant, for example, energy may be used in numerous different ways to produce a whole range of different products. It would be difficult and time-consuming to directly relate expenditure on electricity to the specific products being produced.

How are the different methods used?

Absorption costing is a legal requirement for the valuation of stocks because it satisfies the financial reporting concept of matching costs with sales revenues. Matching is achieved by absorbing factory overheads into stock valuations which are only charged in the profit and loss account when the relevant items are sold. It is therefore the method adopted by most routine product-costing systems.

Marginal costing is appropriate for short-term decision-making, where the knowledge of cost behaviour can maximise contribution to overheads and profits.

Activity-based costing is used to help understand how costs are being incurred. It can give managers important information about which areas of the business are most profitable, and where its future lies.

Marginal costing and **activity-based costing (ABC)** tend to be used on an ad-hoc basis as management techniques to aid decision-making.

QUESTIONS

Cost classification

Consider the following cost categories for Rosemont Ltd, a manufacturer of promotional gifts:

	£000s
Direct labour	670
Administration expenses	350
Factory indirect expenses	375
Direct materials	650
Indirect labour	180
Indirect materials	75
Distribution costs	700

The company applies a 10% mark-up on cost to arrive at a product selling price.

1 Prepare a cost analysis similar to that described by Dr Proctor on page 95.
2 What is the value of:
   i)   prime cost
   ii)   total factory cost
   iii) total cost
   iv)   sales revenue
3 You have calculated the total sales revenue for the firm's entire product range. Given the direct material and labour costs for an individual product, what is the main practical issue in calculating the sales price of an individual product?

Absorption costing

Rosemont Limited has two factory departments: plastic moulding and printing. The indirect costs in respect of these two departments are:

	Total	Plastic moulding	Printing
	£000s	£000s	£000s
Indirect labour	180	70	110
Indirect materials	75	50	25

Indirect factory expenses for both departments are as follows:

Rent and other occupancy costs	£200k
Depreciation of plant and machinery	£175k

The direct labour cost of £650k is in respect of 30 employees in plastic moulding and 10 employees in printing.

The following additional information is also available from the firm's records:

	Plastic moulding	Printing
Value of plant and machinery	£625,000	£250,000
Floor area of factory	200 sq m	120 sq m

Customer order number S1247, for 1,000 personalised paperweights, requires £500 of direct materials, £700 of direct labour in plastic moulding and £400 of direct labour in printing.

On the basis of indirect costs being absorbed as a percentage of direct labour cost, calculate the total factory cost of order number S1247.

Marginal costing

Rosemont Ltd has recently received a sales enquiry that will provide regular work over the next two years.

A bespoke machine costing £5,000 will have to be purchased just for this contract. Monthly revenue of £3,000 would require materials costing £1,000 and the employment of an extra direct worker at a cost of £1,000 per month. Factory overheads are recovered at 100% of direct wages. The order will incur monthly variable costs of £50 for electricity and £100 in respect of plant maintenance. Should Rosemont Ltd accept the order?

Break-even

The Operations Manager at Rosemont Ltd is considering the lease of a van to deliver completed work to customers. Currently customers either pick up their completed order, or arrange collection with a freight carrier. The company deals with 40 customers a month who incur average freight costs of £100 each.

Irrespective of the number of deliveries made, Rosemont incurs monthly costs of £500 for the van lease and £900 for the driver. On average, every delivery incurs £15 in petrol and other running costs.

Continued on page 113

Continued

To be competitive, the Operations Manager believes an average delivery charge of £90 would be appropriate.

1 How many customers must use the delivery service for it to break even?
2 The Operations Manager believes 30 customers a month to be a realistic take-up. What margin of safety would this give?

Activity based costing

Match the following cost drivers to cost pools.

Cost driver	Cost pool
Number of stores requisitions	Personnel dept.
Number of employees	Purchasing dept.
Number of customers	Warehouse
Number of machines	Credit control
Number of purchase orders	Maintenance dept.

Answers

Unit 2: Company Accounts

Fixed assets

1 The forklift truck is a fixed asset because:

- it will be used by Peach Ltd in its business and is not for resale to firm's customers; and
- a number of years will benefit from its use

The asset clearly has continuing value to the business. However, since it has a finite life, its cost must be depreciated over the years that will benefit from its use.

2 Annual depreciation charge =

$$\frac{\text{Cost} - \text{residual value}}{\text{Economic life}}$$

$$= \frac{£9,000 - 0}{5 \text{ years}} = £1,800 \ p.a.$$

3 Net book value =

Cost – Accumulated depreciation to date

After one year = £9,000 – £1,800

= £7,200

After four years = £9,000 – (£1,800 × 4)

= £1,800

Current assets

The following are current assets:

- Stocks: motor cars (£50,000) and motor parts (£3,000) = £53,000
- Debtors: invoices for £3,000
- Cash: Bank £1,500

3 Both workshop machinery and garage premises are not current assets because they are fixed assets.

Liabilities

2 The two categories of creditors distinguish between short-term and longer-term liabilities. This is useful in enabling readers to understand how quickly the business must generate cash to pay them off.

3 In general, day-to-day credit transactions such as trade creditors and liabilities with the tax authorities are the larger items in 'creditors due within one year'. Longer-term sources of finance such as debentures tend to be the larger items under 'creditors due after one year'.

Accounting concepts

1 The four main accounting concepts are: prudence, matching, going concern and consistency.

2 If the going concern concept can no longer be applied, then the likely sale value of assets will have to replace normal valuations if these are lower.

3 Individual valuations:

- Stocks: Category A, £5,000, and Category B, £1,500 (prudence concept determines lower of cost or their market value).
- Debtors: on its own, the first debt would be valued at £9,000 although as part of a category of 'good' debt it may have 1% deducted as a doubtful debt provision (i.e. £8,910). Prudence dictates that the old debt should have nil value.
- Trade creditor: should be valued at £5,000.

Owner's capital

1 *Joan Smith* is an individual; *Joan Smith Ltd* is a corporate entity, recognised separately in law from its owners.

2 The suffix *Ltd* identifies a private limited company; *Plc* identifies a public limited company.

3 Ordinary shares represent the riskiest of a company's share capital, with shareholders usually exercising a say in how the business should be managed. Preference shareholders are usually paid a fixed dividend each year and have little say in business matters.

4 Authorised share capital represents the quota of capital the directors can issue. Issued share capital represents the actual capital invested in the business.

Third-party finance

1 Finance for different time periods:

- *Short-term:* bank overdraft and loans, debt factoring, trade credit
- *Medium-term:* loan stock, HP, leasing, bank loans
- *Long-term:* mortgages, loan stock

2 Finance tied to certain assets: mortgages for specific properties; HP and leases for specific assets such as machines and motor vehicles; debt factors for specified trade debts, creditors for the items being purchased.

The balance sheet

1 Assets = Capital + Liabilities

50,000 = 35,000 + Liabilities

Liabilities = 15,000.

ANSWERS

2 Balance sheet:

	£	£
Fixed assets		
Tangible		40,000
Current assets		
Stocks	15,000	
Debtors	8,000	
Cash at bank and in hand	5,000	
	28,000	
Creditors due within one year	18,000	
Net current assets		10,000
Total assets *less* current liabilities		50,000
Creditors due after more than one year		15,000
Total net assets		35,000
Shareholder funds:		
Share capital		10,000
Retained profits		25,000
Retained profits		35,000

Reporting changes in owners' equity

1 'Realised' gains are those that have actually been made as a result of a business transaction. 'Recognised' gains are merely paper gains, often on the revaluation of a property.
2 Using the headings of 'realised', 'recognised' and 'other changes', categorise the following changes to the capital balance:

- Revaluation gain of £10000 is recognised only.
- 'Issue new shares £10,000' = 'other change'.
- 'Pay a dividend to shareholders of £5,000' = 'other change'.
- Selling goods for a £7,000 profit is a 'realised' gain.
- Paying royalties of £1,000 is a 'realised' loss.

3 'Realised items' are reported in the profit and loss account.

The profit and loss account

1 Gross profit is turnover less cost of sales.
2 Operating profit is gross profit less expenses.
3 Profit retained is profit after tax less dividends to shareholders.

The cash flow statement

1 The cash flow statement shows how the cash balance has changed; the profit and loss account shows how the retained profits has changed.
2 The accrual or matching concept differentiates the two financial reports. The profit and loss account is concerned with occurrences and transactions that change total net assets, whereas the cash flow statement is interested in the receipt and payment of cash.

Regulation of company accounts

1 Government designs and passes laws in the form of the Companies Acts, with which all companies must comply. In addition, the government exercises some influence on the composition of the Financial Reporting Council.
2 The Financial Reporting Council augments the Companies Acts with further accounting rules, and also guidance as regards best accounting practice for a whole range of accounting issues. The Council also oversees the Financial Reporting Review Panel to ensure that published company accounts comply with the various regulations.
3 Auditors have an important role as independent verifiers to ensure that companies keep adequate accounting records and that company accounts are consistent with those records. Their overriding responsibility is to ensure that published accounts give a 'true and fair' view of the financial affairs and the financial performance of the businesses being audited.

Reporting financial performance

1 *Segmental analysis*: where a company has been involved in more than one geographical market, or more than one type of business sector, accounting regulations require turnover, operating profit and net assets to be analysed between the relevant segments.
2 Users of accounts benefit from a knowledge of the underlying business, because industries and markets have different risk and growth prospects, whether these be due to market conditions, technology, social change or political climate.
3 The term 'exceptional items' refers to items that do not normally occur or whose size is unusually large.
4 Exceptional items are liable to distort comparisons between reporting periods, so it is imperative they should be highlighted to prevent wrong conclusions being drawn about the underlying business.
5 Business acquisitions and terminations: All items from turnover to operating profit should be analysed between the continuing operations of the original business, acquisitions and terminations.
6 **By highlighting parts of the business that have been** acquired it is possible to determine the organic growth in the original business. By highlighting continuing operations as opposed to those that have been terminated, it is possible to better extrapolate future performance.

Unit 3: Financial Management

Investment appraisal

Identify whether the following items are one-off or recurring and whether they are in-flows or out-flows of cash.

Item	Incidence	Inflow or Outflow
Sales revenue	Recurring	Inflow
Shopfloor wages	Recurring	Outflow
Purchase of fixed assets	One-off	Outflow
Purchase of stocks for production	Recurring	Outflow
Selling fixed assets at end of project	One-off	Inflow
Tax payable on profits	Recurring	Outflow
Initial product marketing	One-off	Outflow
Royalties paid to product designer	Recurring	Outflow

Supercolour Printers Ltd

1 Annual cash flows from extra sales will be = £500,000 (revenue) - £50,000 (wages) - £100,000 (material) = £350,000.

Payback period:

Year	Cash flow £	Cumulative cash flow £
0	– 400,000	– 400,000
1	350,000	– 50,000
2	350,000	300,000

The payback period is clearly longer than one year but less than two.

Payback period =

1 year + 52 weeks x 50,000/350,000

= 1 year and 7.4 weeks

2 *Net present value:*

Year	Cash flow (£)	Factor	Net present value (£)
0	– 400,000	1	– 400,000
1	350,000	0.8333	291,655
2	350,000	0.6944	243,040
3	350,000	0.5787	202,545
4	350,000	0.4823	168,805
	1,000,000		**506,045**

A positive NPV of £506,045 satisfies the company's investment criteria.

3 *Accounting rate of return:*

Annual profits =

Sales revenue – wages – materials – depreciation

= £500,000 – £50,000 – £100,000 – £400,000/4

= £250,000

Average capital employed = £400,000/2 = £200,000

Accounting rate of return =

$$\frac{\text{Average annual profits}}{\text{Average capital employed}} \times 100\%$$

$$= \frac{£250,000}{£200,000} \times 100\%$$

= 125%

4 Benefits come in the form of annual cost savings. Savings £325,000 less £100,000 running costs.

Payback period:

Year	Cash flow £	Cumulative cash flow £
0	– 300,000	– 300,000
1	225,000	– 75,000
2	225,000	150,000

The payback period is again longer than one year but less than two.

Payback period =

1 year + 52 weeks x 75,000/225,000

= 1 year and 17.3 weeks

5 *Net present value:*

Year	Cash flow (£)	Factor	Net present value (£)
0	– 300,000	1	– 300,000
1	225,000	0.8333	187,493
2	225,000	0.6944	156,240
3	225,000	0.5787	130,208
4	225,000	0.4823	108,518
	600,000		282,459

A positive NPV of £282,459 satisfies the company's investment criteria.

6 *Accounting rate of return:*

Annual profits improvement =

Cutting costs sales revenue – Running costs – Depreciation

= £325,000 – £100,000 – £300,000/4

= £150,000

Average capital employed = £300,000/2 = £150,000

Accounting rate of return =

$$\frac{\text{Average annual profits}}{\text{Average capital employed}} \times 100\%$$

$$= \frac{£150,000}{£150,000} \times 100\% = 100\%$$

7 *Evaluation*:

	Printing press	*Die-cutting machine*
Payback	1 year, 7 weeks	1 year, 17 weeks
Net Present Value	£506,045	£282,459
Accounting rate of return	125%	100%

The printing press would appear to provide the best financial return, as measured by all three appraisal techniques. Although the die-cutting machine provides good returns, the printing press gives a shorter payback period, a higher net book value and a higher accounting rate of return. On a purely financial basis, investment should proceed with the printing press.

Multiple choice

Identify the correct statement:

1 'Payback period' refers to **(b)**: the time taken for the initial investment in a project to be repaid with subsequent cash inflows.
2 'Net present value' refers to **(b)**: for a given project, the present value of all cash inflows *less* the present value of all cash outflows.
3 The most important criteria for the investment of temporary surplus funds **(b)**: low risk.
4 The discount factor used in calculating present values derives directly from **(b)**: the rate of return expected by the firm's investors.
5 Financial appraisal techniques are less appropriate for **(a)**: expenditure to comply with health and safety regulations

Unit 4: Budgets and Forecasts

Limiting factors

Production budget *(see Table A below)*.

Variance analysis

(see Table B below)

3 The only variance of any significance relates to repairs and maintenance expenditure. Most of the year to date variance has occurred during May, but there must be a concern that the overspend trend will continue.

Table A: Production budget

	Jan	Feb	Mar	Apr	May	Jun	Jul	Aug	Sept
B/F	50	50	100	200	250	200	100	50	50
Prod.	50	125	200	200	200	200	200	200	150
Sales	50	75	100	150	250	300	250	200	150
C/F	50	100	200	250	200	100	50	50	50

From February, production will have to be increased above current demand levels in readiness for the peak period.

Table B: Variances

	May			Year to date		
	Actual	Budget	Variance	Actual	Budget	Variance
Direct wages	11.5	12.0	0.5	62.1	63.0	0.9
Salaries	5.9	6.0	0.1	29.9	30.0	0.1
Training	0.8	0.5	− 0.3	1.8	2.5	0.7
Welfare	0.2	0.3	0.1	1.2	1.5	0.3
Repairs & M.	5.5	2.5	− 3.0	17.1	12.5	-4.6
Consumables	1.8	1.5	− 0.3	7.4	7.5	0.1
Depreciation	14.3	14.5	0.2	72.1	72.5	0.4
Total	40.0	37.3	− 2.7	191.6	189.5	− 2.1

4 Details should be obtained of the repairs and related costs to help answer the following questions: Is the reporting accurate? Were the costs justified? Were they properly authorised? Was there a more cost effective solution? What are the implications for future spend?

Cash flow forecast

1 Before constructing the cash flow forecast, it is worth detailing out sales and purchases before phasing the actual cash transaction (*see Table C below*).

Jit Baktar cash flow forecast, May to October (*see Table D below*).

2 The cash forecast shows that Jit's business should have adequate finance during its first six months of trading as the cash balance is forecast to be positive throughout the period. A business startup should have a cash forecast prepared for a longer period, particularly when individual periods still see payments in excess of receipts and a negative cash balance may arise. However, if Jit's business is able to continue growing at its current rate, revenues should grow at a faster rate than payments.

Table C: Sales and purchases, May to October

	May	Jun	Jul	Aug	Sept	Oct
	£	£	£	£	£	£
Service contracts	200	400	600	800	1,000	1,200
Equipment sales	2,000	3,000	4,000	5,000	6,000	7,000
Purchases	5,000	2,100	2,800	3,500	4,200	4,900

Table D: Cash flow forecast, May to October

	May	Jun	Jul	Aug	Sept	Oct
	£	£	£	£	£	£
Receipts						
Capital from Jit	5,000					
Loan	8,000					
Service contracts		200	400	600	800	1,000
Sales receipts		2,000	3,000	4,000	5,000	6,000
Total receipts	13,000	2,200	3,400	4,600	5,800	7,000
Payments:						
Salaries					1,250	1,250
Rent and rates	300	300	300	300	300	300
Sundries	100	100	100	100	100	100
Purchase of materials	5,000	2,100	2,800		3,500	4,200
Drawings	1,000	1,000	1,000	1,000	2,000	2,000
Total payments	6,400	3,500	4,200	1,400	7,150	7,850
Receipts minus payments	6,600	– 1,300	-800	3,200	– 1,350	– 850
Balance brought forward	0	6,600	5,300	4,500	7,700	6,350
Balance carried forward	**6,600**	**5,300**	**4,500**	**7,700**	**6,350**	**5,500**

Unit 5: Ratio Analysis

1 *See Table E.*

2 *Deteriorated (DET) or Improved (IMP):*

	Red	Blue
Gross margin %	DET	DET
Operating margin %	DET	DET
Return on capital employed	DET	DET
Stock turnover	DET	IMP
Debtor days	DET	DET
Current ratio	DET	IMP
Margin of safety	DET	DET

3 Red Ltd experienced a fall in operating profit despite an increase in turnover because all cost categories (cost of sales, distribution and administration) increased by an even greater percentage. With costs being a bigger proportion of the selling price, clearly Red Ltd is experiencing pricing pressures in the marketplace. If the trend continues, the outlook for future profitability is not good.

Blue Ltd produced a reduced operating profit largely as a result of costs incurred in reorganising the distribution function. Without this exceptional item, operating profits would have increased by £250,000 over Year 1, giving a profit margin of 19.1% instead of the 12.7% actually achieved. Although there was a slight decrease in the gross profit margin, distribution costs and administration expenses fell as a percentage of sales. The outlook for future profitability is good, with the next year benefiting from a full year of reduced distribution costs.

4 From our knowledge of the balance sheet, explained in Unit 2, we know that Capital = Assets – Liabilities.

As capital changed in Year 2 (Red Ltd reduced by £30k, Blue Ltd increased by £200k), then assets *less* liabilities had to change by similar amounts. But a change in short-term debt would have been necessary if changes to assets and liabilities (other than short-term debt) did not equal the change in

Table E

	Red Ltd		Blue Ltd	
	Year 1	Year 2	Year 1	Year 2
i) Gross margin %	3,850/7,900 = 48.7%	3,700/8,000 = 46.25%	2,250/4,900 = 45.9%	2,450/5,500 = 44.5%
ii) Operating margin %	750/7,900 = 9.5%	350/ 8,000 = 4.4%	800/4,900 = 16.3%	700/5,500 = 12.7%
iii) Return on capital employed	2,625 + 1,200 – 100 = 3,725 750/3,725 = 20.1%	2,595 + 1,305 = 3,900 350/3,900 = 9.0%	1,900 + 2,200 –50 = 4,050 800/4,050 = 19.8%	2,100 + 2,350 = 4,450 700/4,450 = 15.7%
iv) Stock turnover	4,050/600 = 6.75	4,300/800 = 5.38	2,650/550 = 4.82	3,050/500 = 6.1
v) Debtor days	25 x 365/7,900 = 1 day	50 x 365/ 8,000 = 2 days	700 x 365/ 4,900 = 52 days	1,050 x 365/5,500 = 70 days
vi) Current ratio	725/ 900 = 0.81	850/1,505 = 0.56	1,300/900 = 1.44	1,550/1,000 = 1.55
vii) Interest cover	750/250 = 3.75	350/250 = 1.40	800/250 = 3.2	700/300 = 2.33

capital. To maintain the balance sheet formula, if a particular liability increased, then either assets increased or the other liabilities decreased. Hence we need to scan the Year 2 balance sheets of each company for any such instances.

The increased short-term borrowings for Red Ltd arose mainly as a result of a fall in long-term debt (i.e. 500k moving into its last year before repayment is due), but also as a result of increased stocks. Short-term borrowings for Blue Ltd increased, mainly because debtors increased by £350,000. We can deduce that this was either because Blue Ltd allowed its customers more credit as an incentive to increase sales, or the company exercised less control to ensure that customers paid on time.

5   Red Ltd appears to be experiencing a relatively poor trading performance which may lead to future operating losses. Current operating profits provide only a small margin of safety for the payment of debt interest and even with a reduced dividend, Year 2 dividends exceeded the amount of post-tax profit generated in the year. To exacerbate the situation, a growing proportion of debt is falling due for repayment in the near future. The company needs to address its trading performance, exercise greater control over its stock levels and raise additional finance to tide itself over what appears to be a difficult period.

Blue Ltd is in a far better position, as it should benefit further from measures already taken to improve its distribution operations. The company's finances appear to be fairly sound, although a review of its credit control procedures would be appropriate.

6   Red Ltd would appear to be the retailer and Blue Ltd the engineering firm. The best evidence of this is to be found in the current assets section of the balance sheet. As we would expect of a retailer, Red Ltd has very few debtors and as a result has a low current ratio.

Unit 6: Costs and Decision-making

Cost classification

	£000s	£000s
Direct materials		650
Direct labour		670
Prime cost		1,320
Factory overheads:		
Indirect materials	75	
Indirect labour	180	
Indirect expenses	375	630
Total factory cost		1,950
Distribution costs		700
Administration expenses		350
Total cost		3,000
Profit		300
Sales revenue		3,300

- Prime cost is £1,320,000
- Total factory cost is £1,950,000.
- Total cost is £3,000,000.
- Sales revenue is £3,300,000.

The difficulty with calculating the selling price of an individual product lies in how much of the indirect costs (including distribution and administration) should be shouldered by each product.

Absorption costing (See Table F)

Marginal costing

Deciding whether or not to accept a customer order is a classic situation for the application of marginal costing. The important issue is to identify changes to costs and revenues as a result of accepting the order.

As the project's time-scale is relatively short, it is possible to consider the relevant cash flows without the complications of discounted cash flow:

Table F: Cost schedule

	Total £000	Plastic moulding £000	Printing £000
Direct labour	650.0	487.5	162.5
Indirect costs:			
Indirect labour	180	70	110
Indirect materials	75	50	25
Rent[1]	200	125	75
Depreciation[2]	175	125	50
Total	630	370	260
Percentage of direct labour		75.9%	160%

Notes
Apportionment based on:
1 Floor area
2 Plant value

Order no S1247: Factory cost	% of Direct Labour	£
Direct material		500.00
Direct labour – Plastic moulding		700.00
Direct labour – Printing		400.00
Indirect cost – Plastic moulding	75.9%	531.30
Indirect cost – Printing	160.0%	640.00
Total factory cost		2,771.30

Over the 2 years:

	£
Investment in new machine	– 5,000
Sales revenue (£3,000 x 24)	72,000
Materials (£1,000 x 24)	– 24,000
Labour (£1,000 x 24)	– 24,000
Variable expenses (£150 x 24)	– 3,600
Contribution	15,400

Note: The overhead that would be recovered by the firm's costing system is not a relevant cost – it is merely a book entry that has arisen because absorption costing systems spread costs all of a firm's output.

Break-even

Contribution per delivery = Sales price – Variable cost

Contribution per delivery = £90 – £15 = £75
Break-even = Fixed cost/ Contribution per delivery
= £1,400/ £75
= 19 deliveries

Margin of safety =

$$\frac{\text{Actual nos.* – Break-even nos.}}{\text{Break-even nos.}}$$

= (30 – 19)/19

= 58%

* In this case anticipated.

Activity-based costing

Cost drivers matched to cost pools:

Cost driver	Cost pool
No. of stores requisitions	Warehouse
No. of employees	Personnel dept.
No. of customers	Credit control
No.of machines	Maintenance dept.
No. of purchase orders	Purchasing dept.

Glossary of terms

The following glossary gives definitions of terms and vocabulary not specifically defined in the text.

Absorption costing Enables the total cost of a product to be calculated, including overheads.

Administration expenses Costs that are not associated with producing and delivering goods and services to the customer, e.g. preparing financial accounts for the company.

Balance sheet A snapshot of a firm's assets, liabilities and sources of capital at a moment in time.

Benchmark An appropriate measure of comparison, e.g. last year's wage bill would be a benchmark against which to measure this year's.

Capital expenditure authorisation A formal process for authorising capital expenditure, usually including the sanction of senior management.

Catalyst A change agent which speeds up a process.

Consumables Items that are difficult to measure or of low value that are consumed as part of the production process.

Control tool A mechanism for controlling an activity, e.g. a budgetary control system compares actual performance against budget, enabling management to take action as appropriate.

Corporation tax Taxes paid on business profits.

Cost centre A part of the business organisation for which costs are collected, e.g. the marketing department.

Cost driver The reason why a cost is incurred.

Cost object The item for which costs are being collected, i.e. either a cost unit or a cost centre.

Cost of sales The cost of making the products and services sold to customers.

Delivery lead times The time between placing an order and receiving the goods.

Discount factor Derived from the firm's cost of money; used to convert future cash flows into present values.

Discretionary Not essential, but commercially justifiable, e.g. the purchase of a new delivery vehicle.

Distribution costs The cost of getting the firm's product from the factory to the customer.

Dividend Payment to shareholders out of company profits.

Economic batch quantities The buying quantity that gives best value, taking into account expenses such as storage costs.

Equity The capital provided by ordinary shareholders, including retained profits.

Finance lease Form of finance for a fixed asset which does not confer legal ownership of the item.

Flexing Adjustment of a cost budget to reflect actual production or sales volumes.

Loan stock Loans that can be bought and sold in the same way as shares in a company.

Net wealth The value of assets *less* liabilities.

Nominal value The value at which a share is recorded in the accounting records.

Objectives The stated aim or purpose of the business.

Operating activities The business of satisfying customer needs as opposed to incidentals such as earning interest on surplus cash.

Opportunity cost The benefit foregone as a result of taking an alternative option.

Profit centre A part of the business organisation for which both sales revenues and costs are collected and reported.

Production overheads Indirect costs incurred by the production facility.

Ratio The relationship between one business variable and another, e.g. sales revenue per employee.

Residual value The value of an asset at the end of its useful life, e.g. a company car after three years.

Return on capital employed (ROCE) Profit before interest, expressed as a percentage of capital employed.

Royalty payments Amounts paid to the designer/inventor of a product or production process.

Share premium The difference between the amount received and the nominal value when a company issues new shares.

Solvency Ability to pay wages, supplier's bills and other obligations as they fall due.

Strategies The means by which the firm will attain its objectives, e.g. to standardise products to become the lowest-cost producer.

Tangible Physical items.

Third-party finance Funds provided by individuals and organisations external to a business.

Working capital The financial resources that enable a firm to operate on a day-to-day basis, e.g. having stock to sell, the ability to give customers credit and having cash to pay bills as they fall due.

Index